TABLE OF CONTENTS

Introduction	i
10 Actionable KPI Designs	6
10 Ways to Display Variance with Bar Charts	17
11 Ways to Compare Two Measures	28
18 Ways to Visualize Bar Charts	40
60 Ways to Visualize Time	59

INTRODUCTION

Hey there! You're holding a book that's all about making your journey into the world of data visualization as smooth and practical as possible.

Here are some tips for how to get the most out of this book:

1. Write All Over It

When an idea clicks, jot down how you might use it or scribble down any questions that pop up. This book will become a personalized guide that grows with your skills.

2. Dog-Ear the Essentials

Find a page that is super important? Fold the corner!

3. Mark Your Experiments

Tried using a specific chart type or technique? Make a note of what worked and what didn't right next to the idea.

4. Share Your Thoughts

Found a section incredibly insightful or perhaps a bit confusing? Write your thoughts in the margins. These comments are great for revisiting concepts or for discussions with colleagues.

5. Expand the Content

Is there something you wish was covered or something you've experimented with that could be added? Use the blank spaces to add your insights or additional research.

6. Track Your Progress

At the end of each chapter, jot down a few bullet points about what you've learned or practiced. Watching your progress can be incredibly satisfying and motivating!

Your Experience Matters!

This book is meant to be a living tool, evolving as you do. Don't worry about keeping it pristine—your interaction is what will breathe life into these pages, turning "Charting Made Easy" into a guide tailored just for you.

So, what are you waiting for? Dive in, build some charts, and let's pave your path to mastering data visualization together!

10
KPI DESIGNS
THAT SHOW WHEN YOU NEED TO TAKE ACTION

01

SALES
130,388,128
+3.9% vs. PY

Use a big number to summarize a metric.

It's useful to provide context to allow comparison to another value.

02

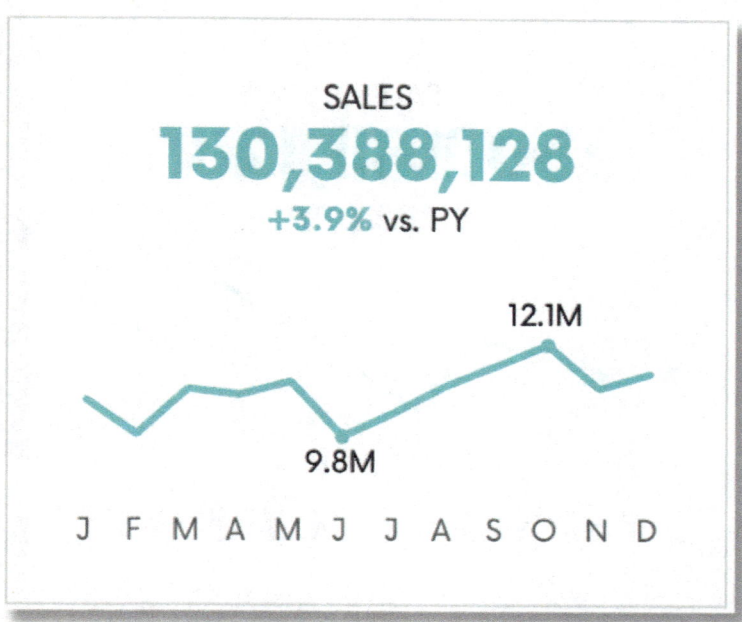

Add even more context to your big number by including a line chart to show the overall trend.

03

Provide additional context by adding a second line for the comparison period.

04

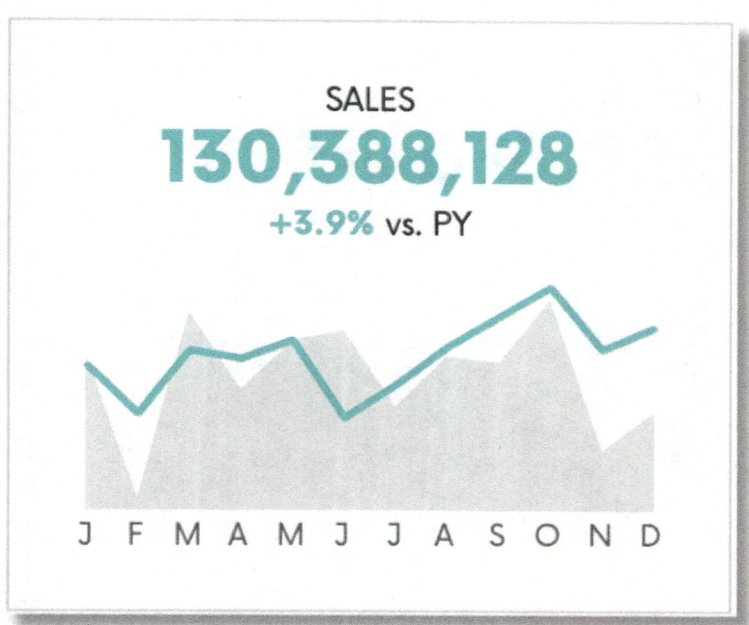

A combination of line and area chart makes your focus metric stand out.

05

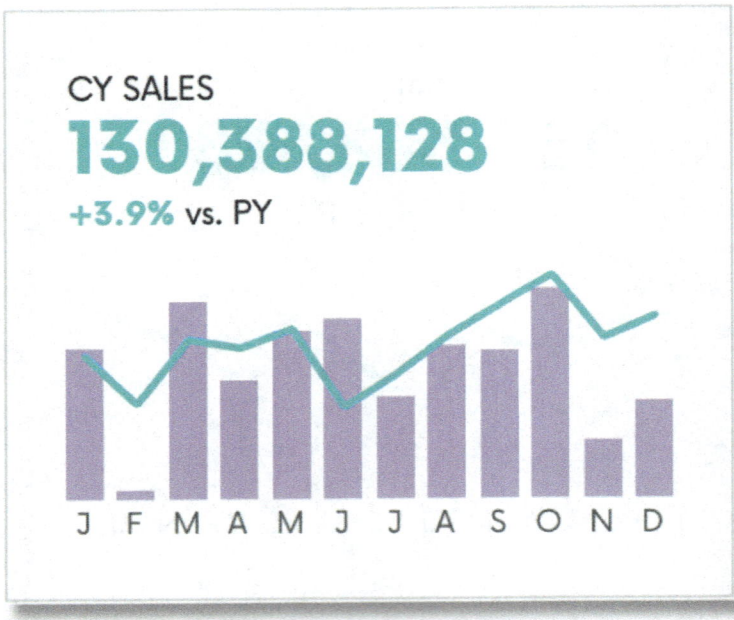

Using a combined bar and line chart allows for quick comparisons of current and prior year.

06

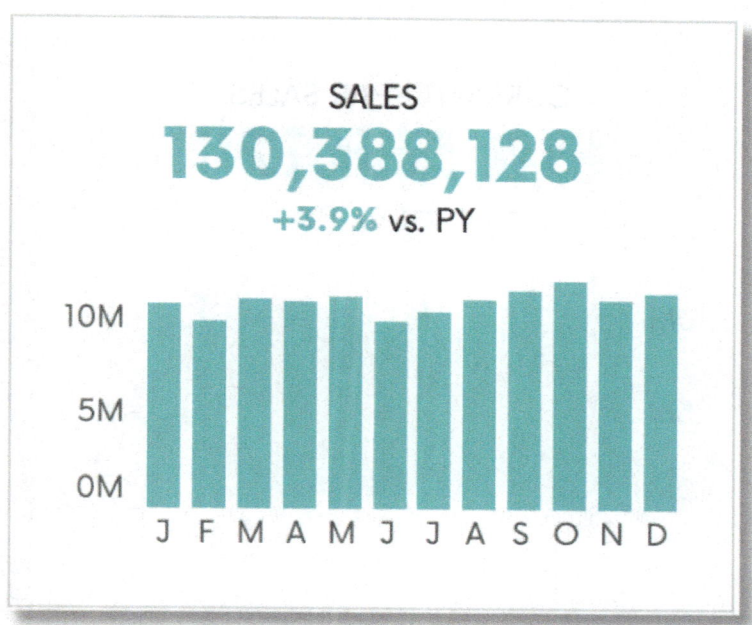

Support your large KPI number with a bar chart to show the trend

07

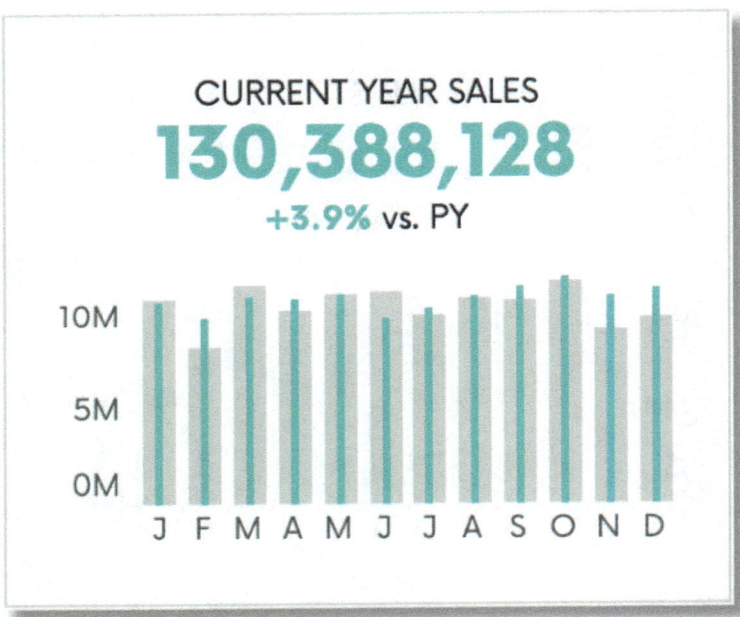

You can use a bar-in-bar chart to show comparisons of the two periods.

08

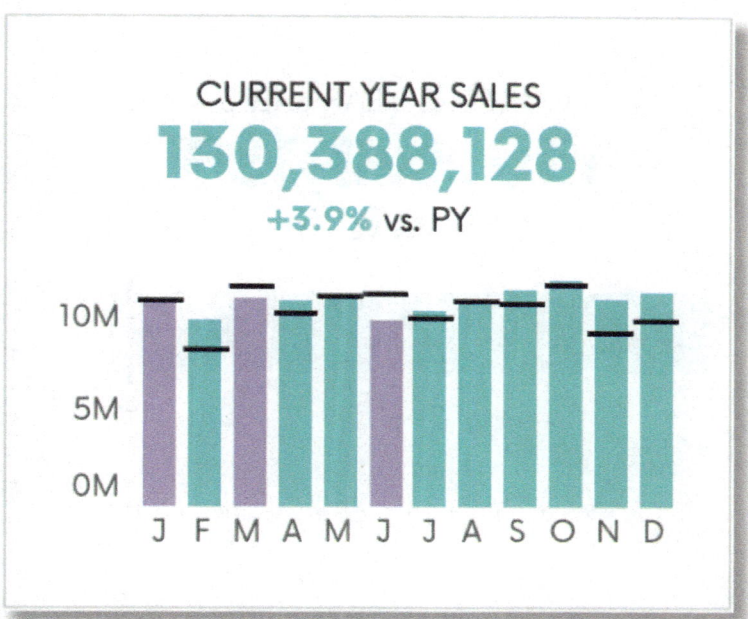

Add reference lines and conditional formatting to your bar chart to quickly show performance against a second metric.

09

CURRENT YEAR SALES
130,388,128
+3.9% vs. PY

Visually support your big number by using a single bar with reference line.

Color the bar by above or below the target.

10

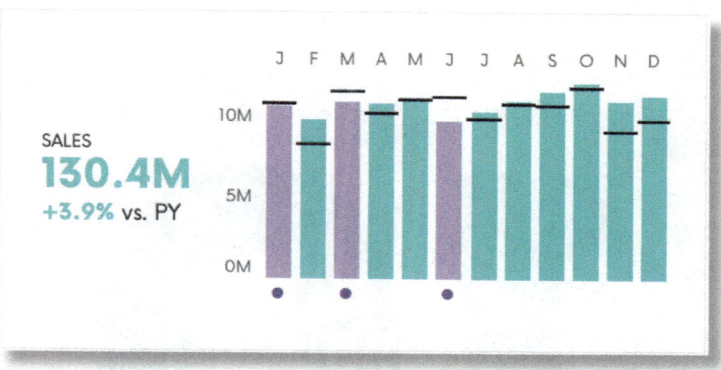

Combine several of the previous examples.

Move the big number to the left.

Use the bar chart with the comparison line.

Add a dot for additional focus on those missing the target.

10
WAYS TO DISPLAY VARIANCE WITH BAR CHARTS

01

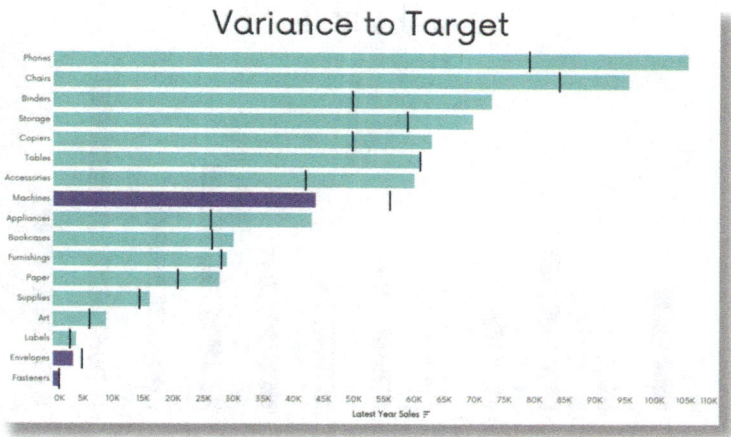

Use reference lines and conditional formatting to quickly show performance against a second metric.

02

Side by Side

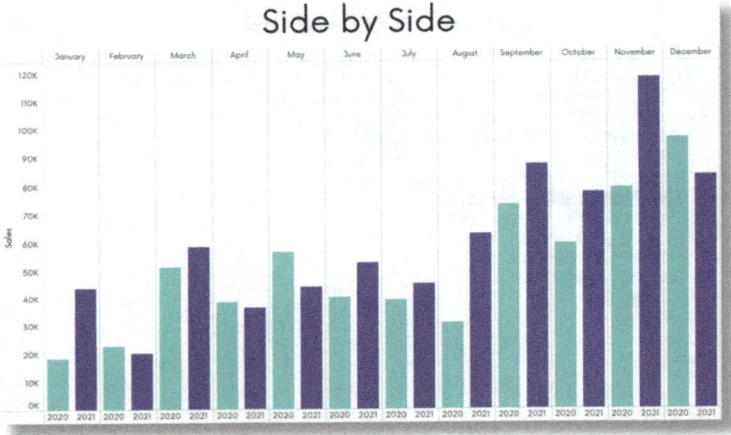

Change the order of your dimension members to compare two years for each month.

03

Bar in Bar

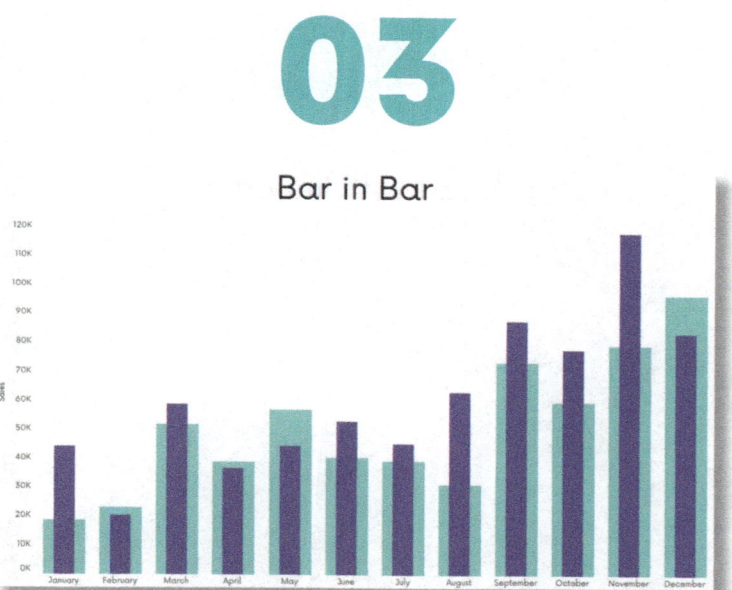

Stack bars on top of each other for easy comparison of two periods.

04

Bar Chart with Indicator

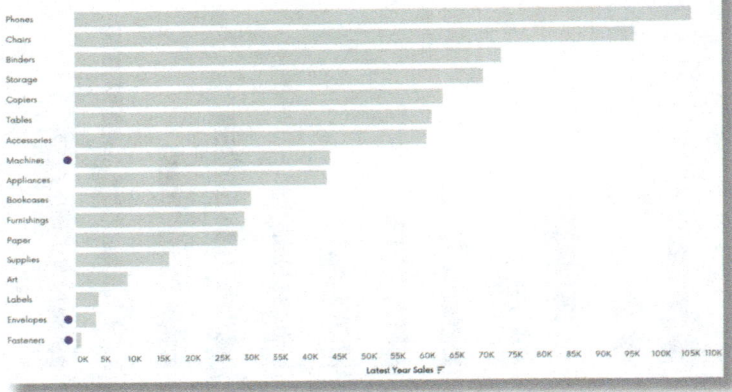

Add an indicator to your bar chart to draw attention to specific dimension members or data points.

05

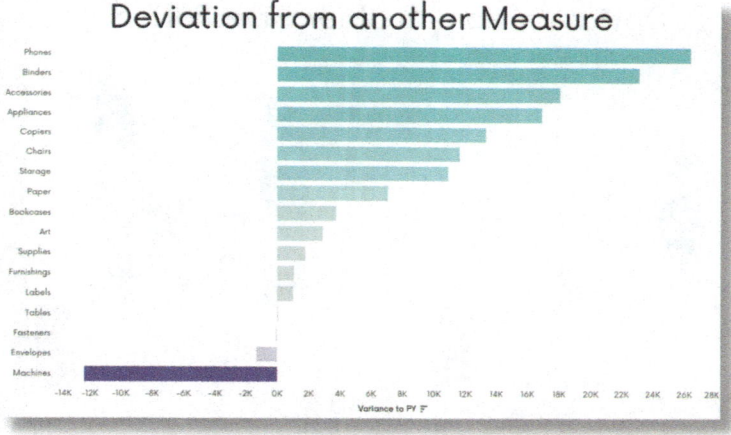

Highlight the variance against a chosen measure using color.

Deviation from another Time Period

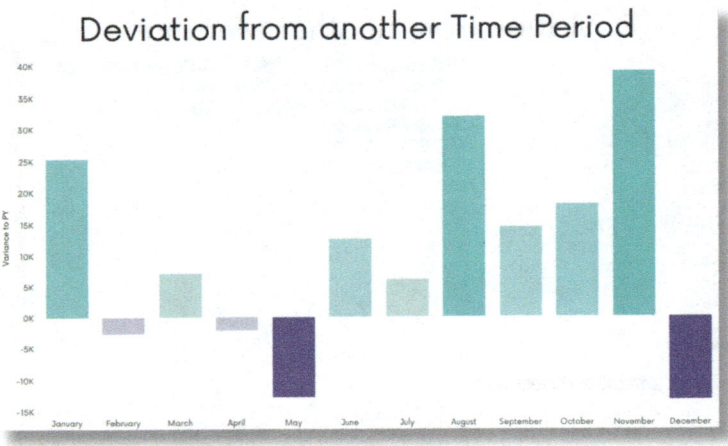

Highlight the variance from a comparison period using color in a diverging bar chart.

Floating Bar Chart

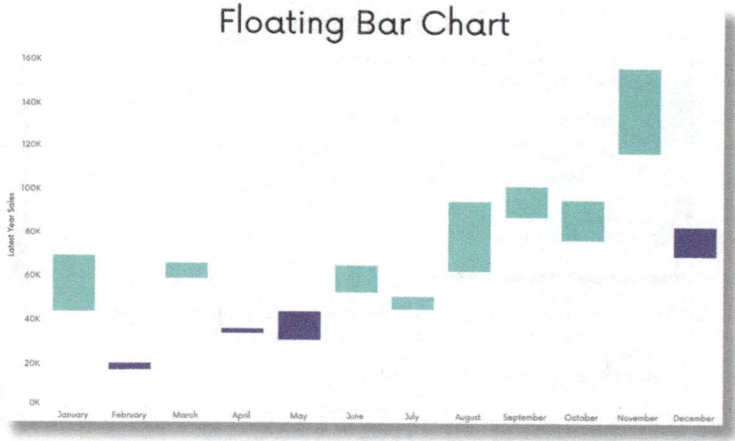

Show the difference between two periods by showing the range of the data for each point in time and coloring the magnitude of the difference.

08

Bullet Graph

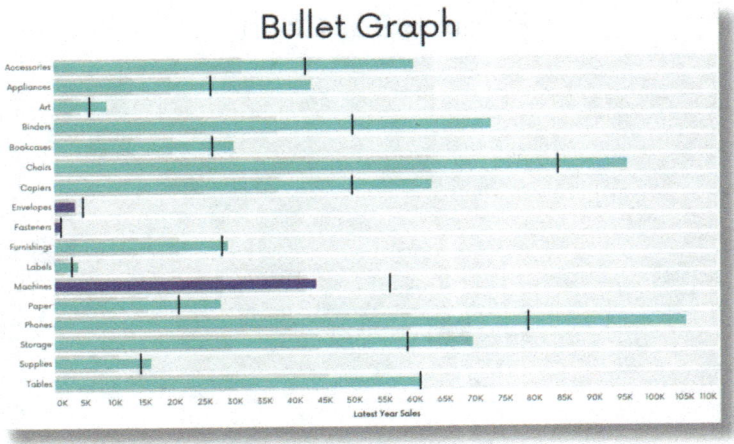

Create a bullet graph by adding reference bands to show 50%, 75%, and 100% of the target.

Add a reference line at the target for emphasis.

09

Sparkbars

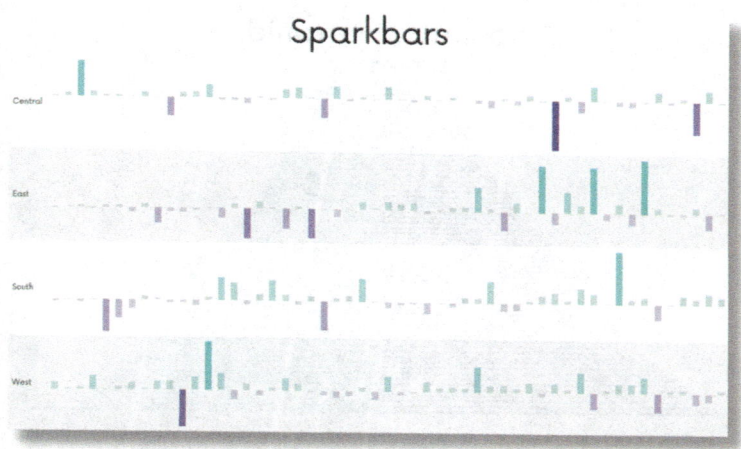

Use a compact bar chart similar to a sparkline.

Useful for focusing trends over time rather than across dimensions.

Works especially well for data the has negative and positive values.

10

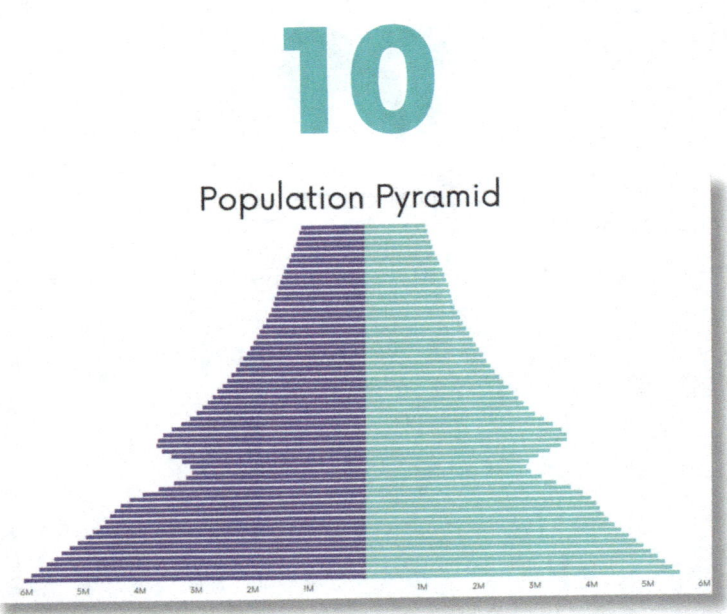

Population Pyramid

Use a diverging bar chart to visualize one metric over time across two dimension members

11

WAYS TO COMPARE
TWO MEASURES

01

PAIRED BAR CHART

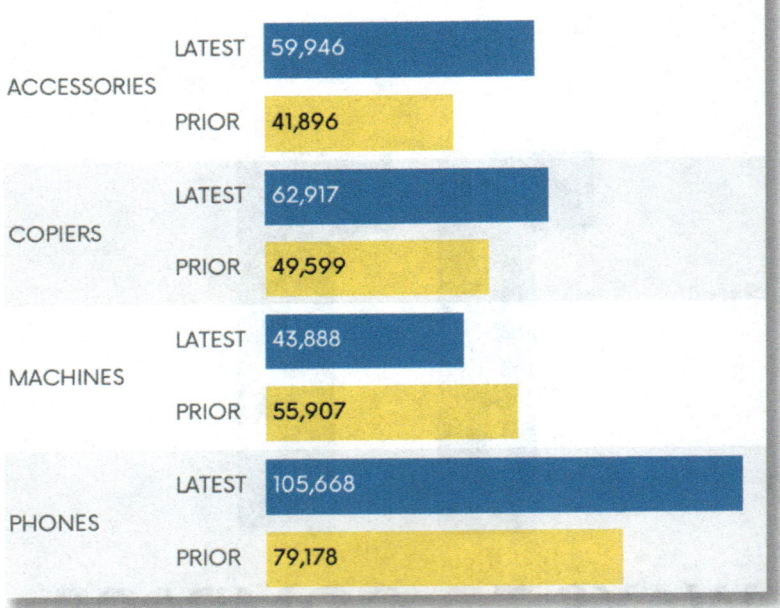

Compare two periods for each dimension member using a paired bar chart.

Label the bars for precision and context.

02

BAR IN BAR

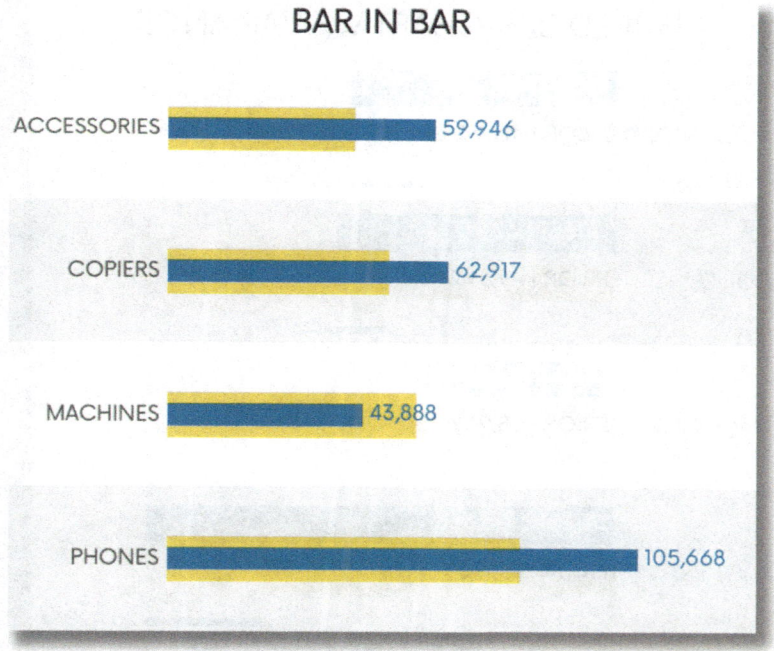

Add a label to a bar in bar chart on the focus metric to give context of magnitude.

03

PAIRED BAR CHART w/ VARIANCE

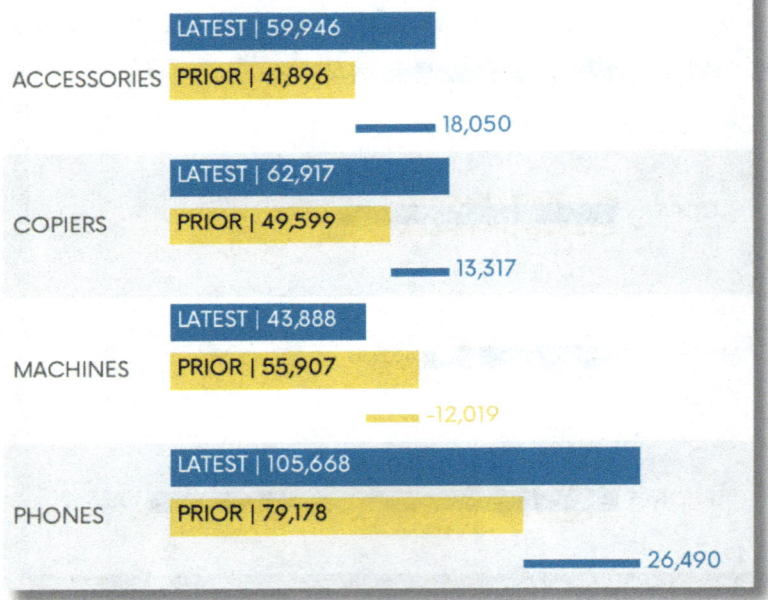

Add a separate labeled bar showing the variance between two periods.

04

LINE CHART

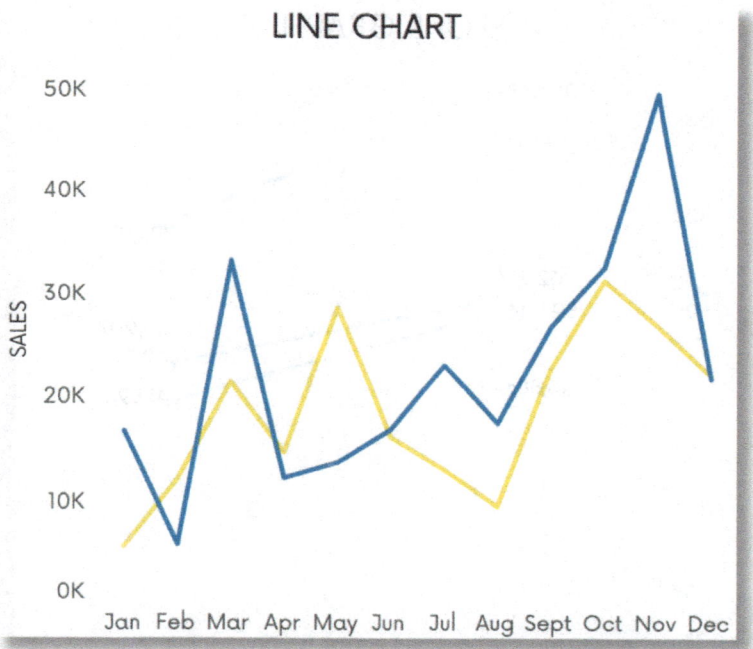

Use colored lines to show trends over time and allow for quick comparison between two periods.

05

SLOPE GRAPH

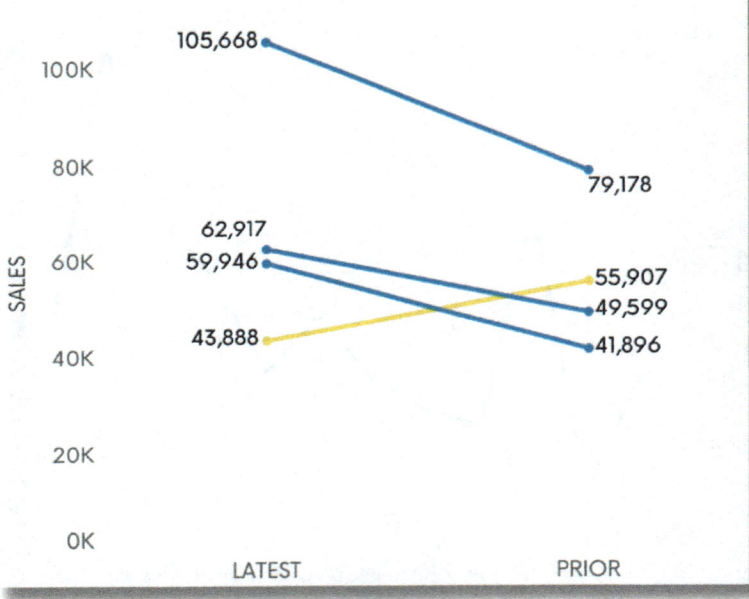

Make comparison of two periods simple using a labeled, colored slope chart

06

BARBELL

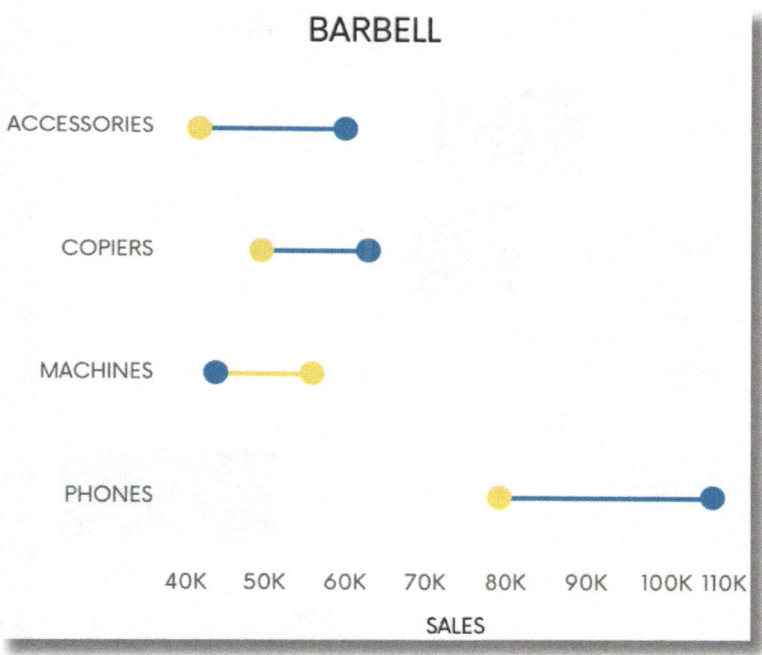

Use circle to represent each period, connect them with a line and color the line the same as the circle with the largest value.

07

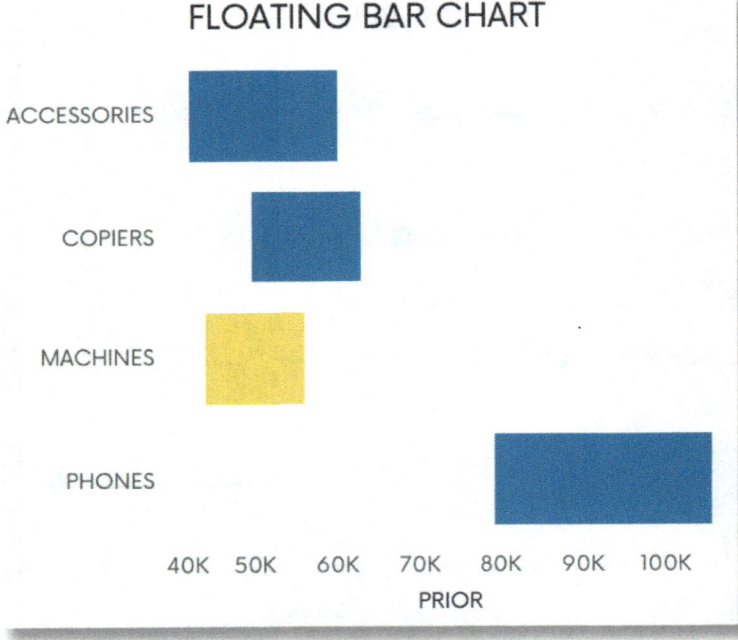

Each side of the bar represents one of the two values. Then compare one period against the other, showing size difference via bar length.

Color the bar by the period with the higher value.

08

COMET CHART

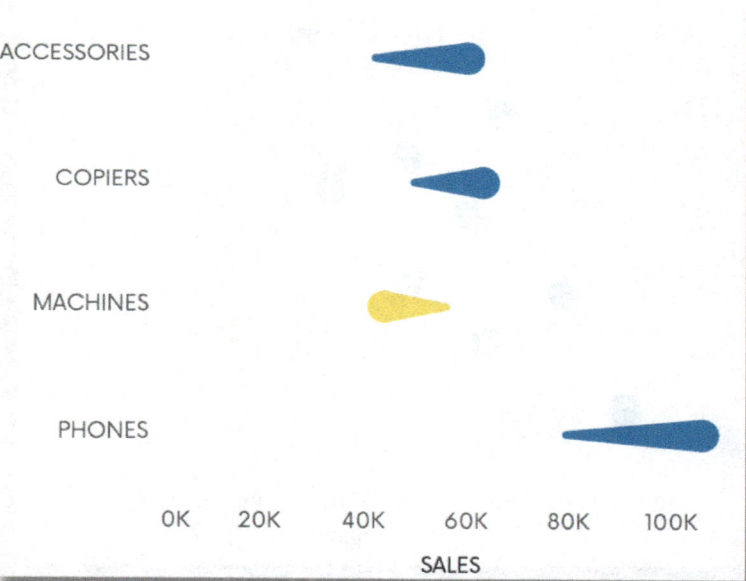

The direction and color of the comet indicate which period had higher sales.

09

SCATTERPLOT

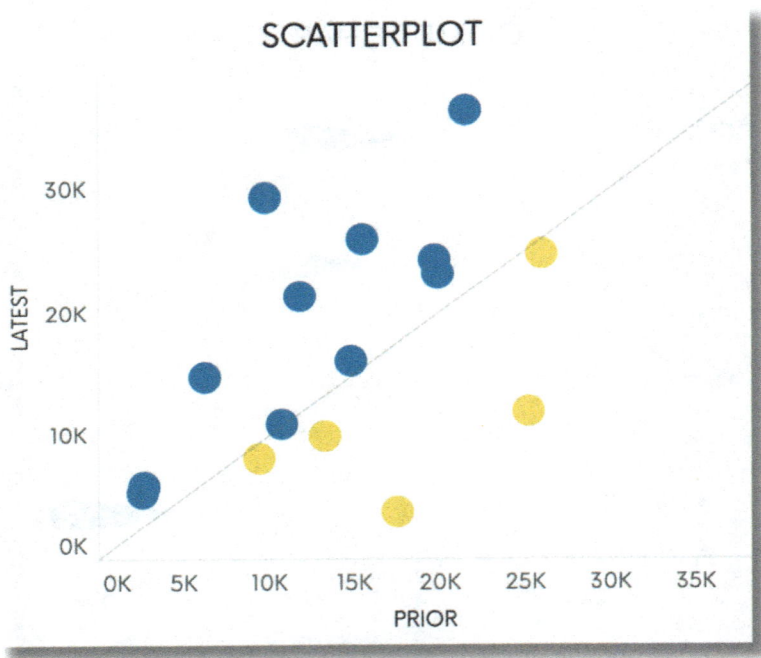

Add a 45° reference line to your scatterplot to clearly show which data points fall higher or lower for one value vs. another.

10

X/Y HEATMAP

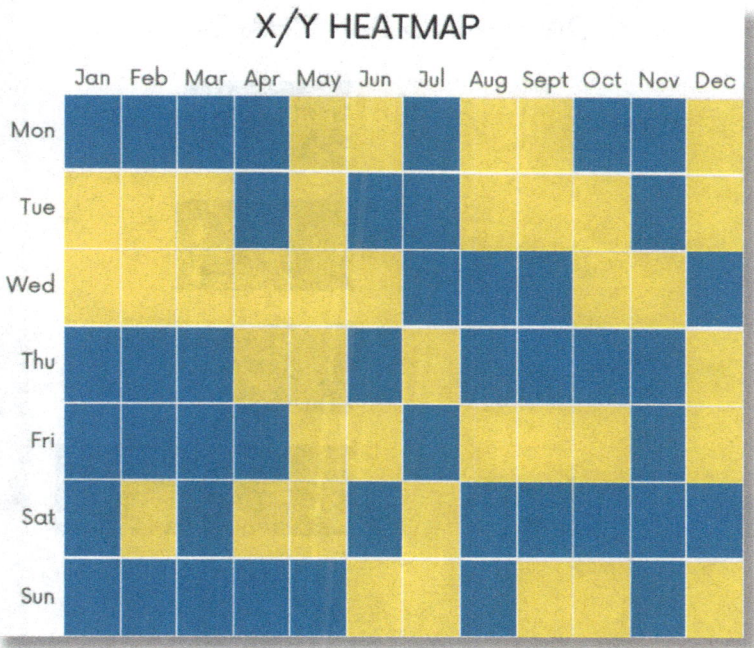

Use a heatmap to show the pattern in your data, highlighting which of the two periods has a larger value for each weekday & month combination

11

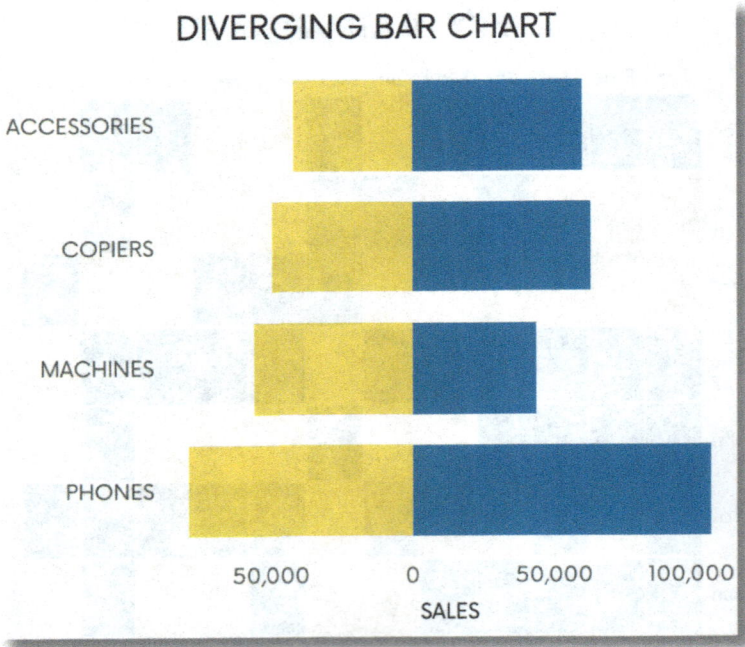

Show sales results for two periods from a central point. One time period points to the left, the other to the right.

18

WAYS TO VISUALIZE
BAR CHARTS

Inspired by Rosa Mariana de Leon-Escribano

01

BAR CHART

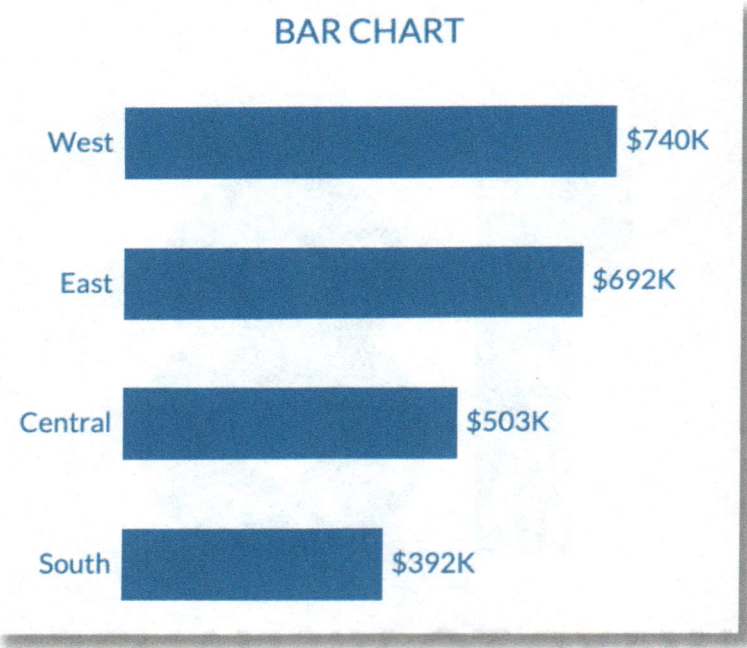

Use a single color and label each bar for context.

02

OUTLINE BAR CHART

Region	Value
West	$740K
East	$692K
Central	$503K
South	$392K

Simplify your bars by using only an outline and centering labels.

03

ROUNDED BAR CHART

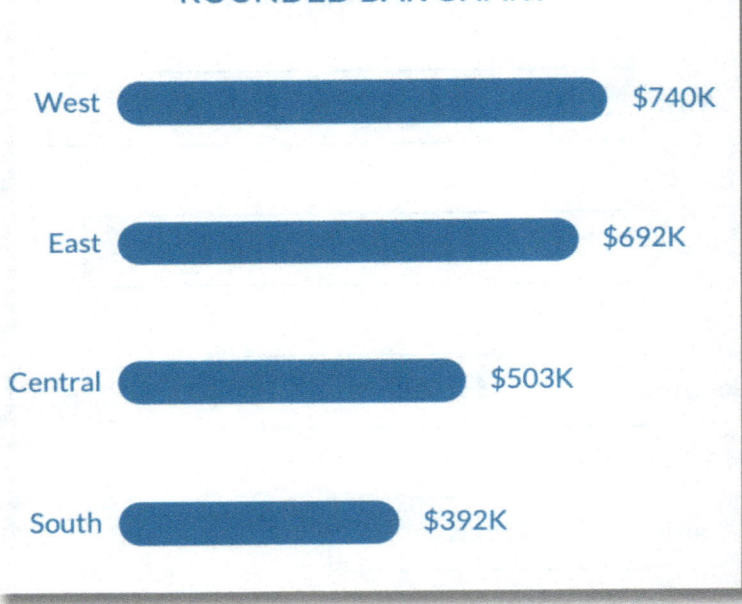

Rounded edges give your bars a more 'designed' look.

Include labels to maintain precision.

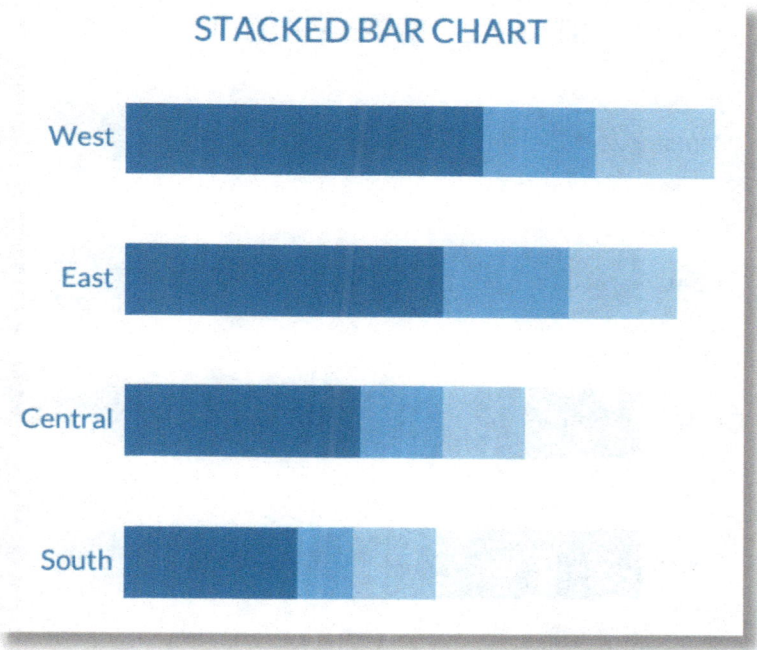

Combine multiple dimension members in a stacked bar chart to show how the different parts compare.

05

STACKED BAR CHART II

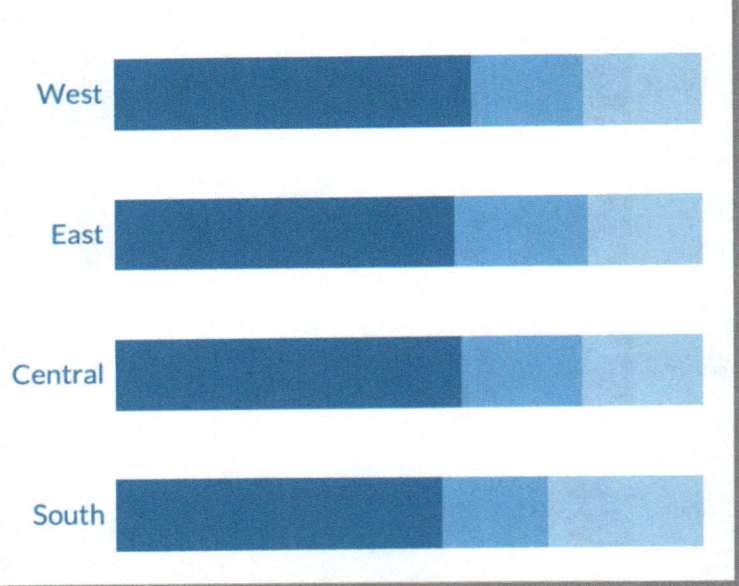

Stacking the bars as a percent of total adds more context by allowing viewers to compare proportions.

This also allows for easy to understand comparisons of the colors across a series of dimensions.

06

DIVERGENT BAR CHART

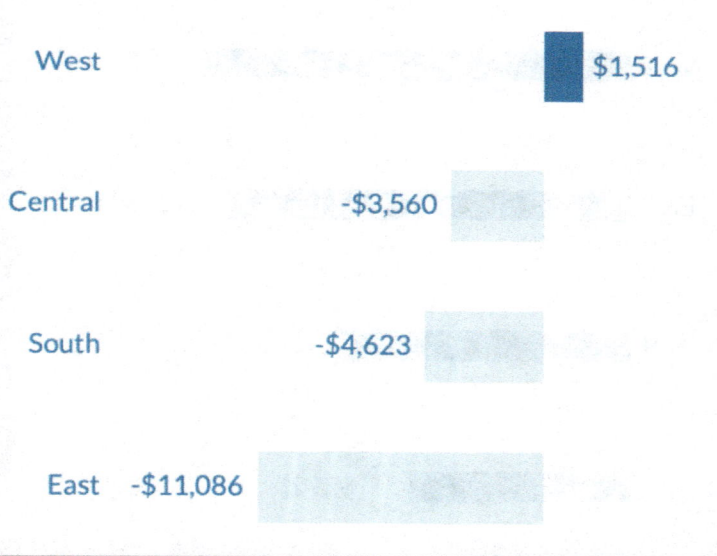

Bars that diverge from a baseline are colored based on the value of that difference.

07

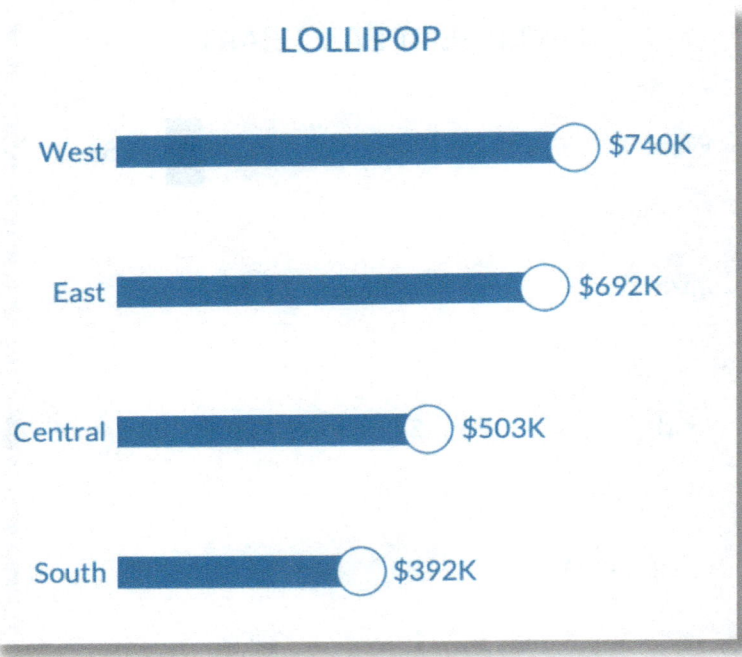

Adding a circle to the end of a bar chart helps draw attention to its length.

A label adds precision.

08

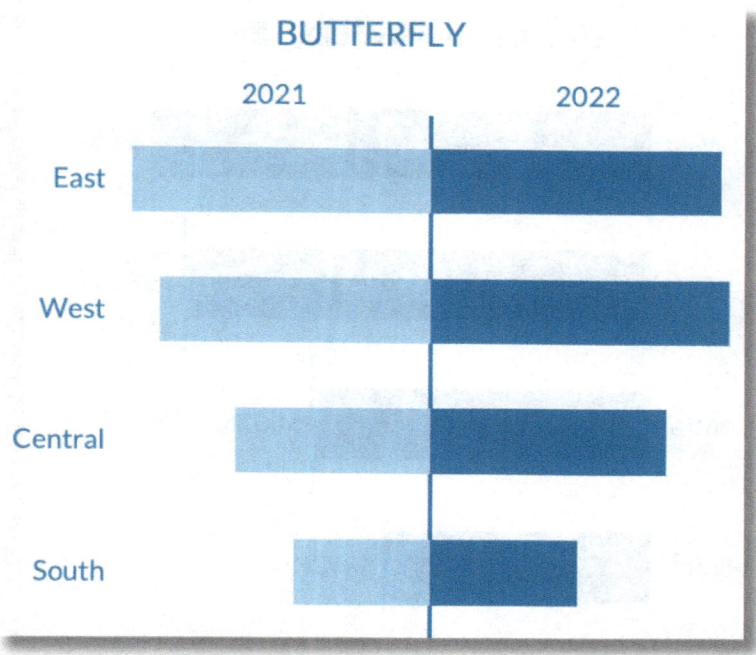

Compare two periods using color and a butterfly chart with a common central baseline.

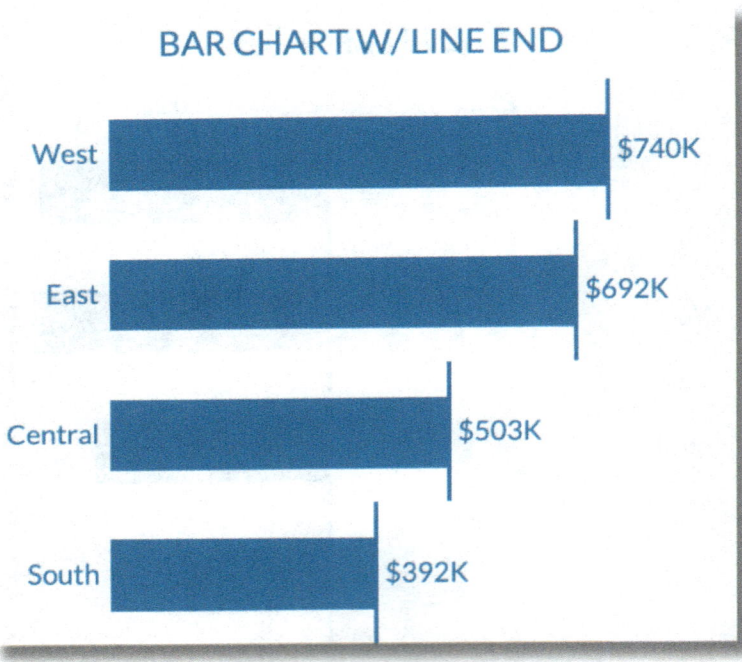

Add a reference line at the end of each bar to add a visual end point.

Label your bar for precision.

10

BULLET GRAPH

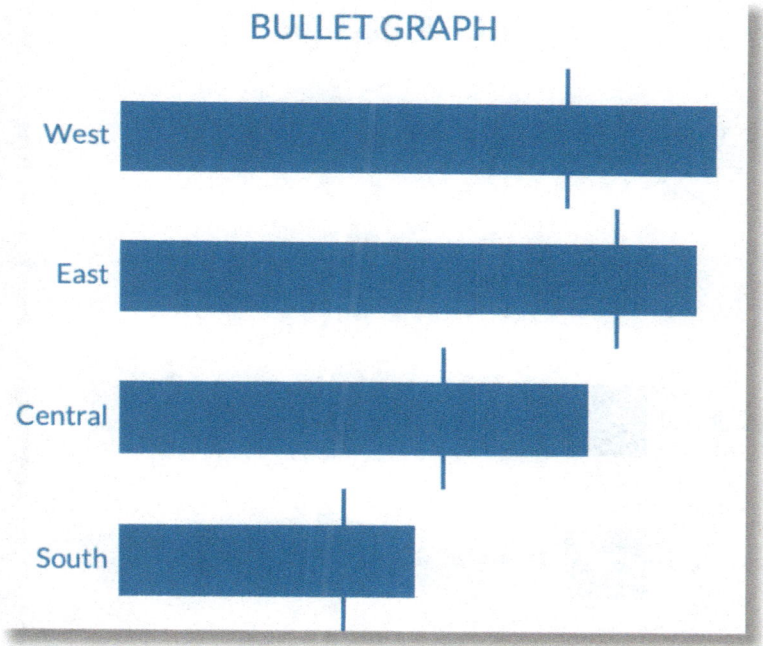

Compare a metric against a target using reference lines for each bar.

PROGRESS BAR

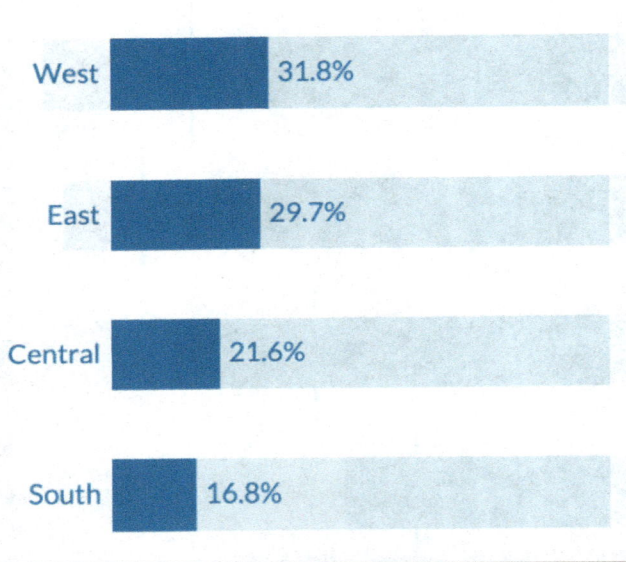

Show actual results vs a 100% target in a progress bar.

12

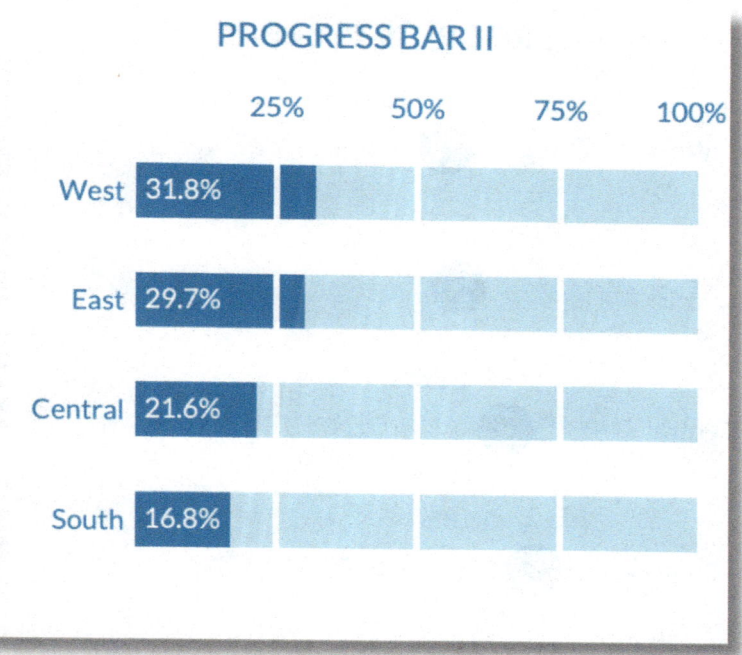

Divide your progress bar into equal chunks for quick comparison of actual vs target.

13

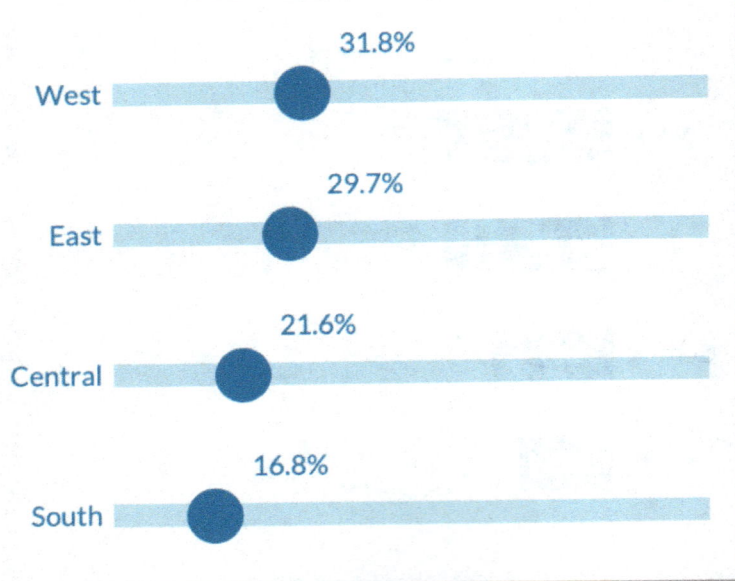

Use a circle on a thin bar to show progress against a 100% target.

14

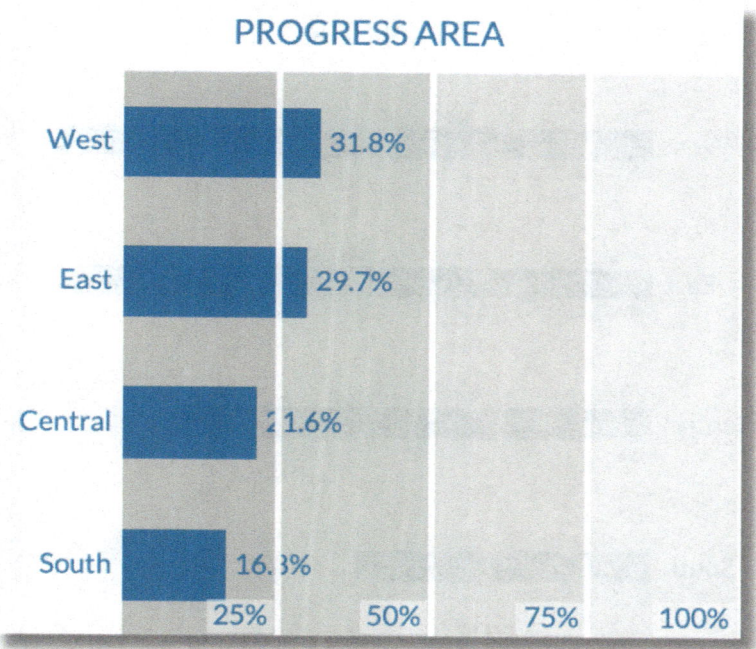

Reference bands at regular intervals help show performance against targets.

15

BAR IN BAR

Compare two metrics simply by using color on a bar in bar chart

16

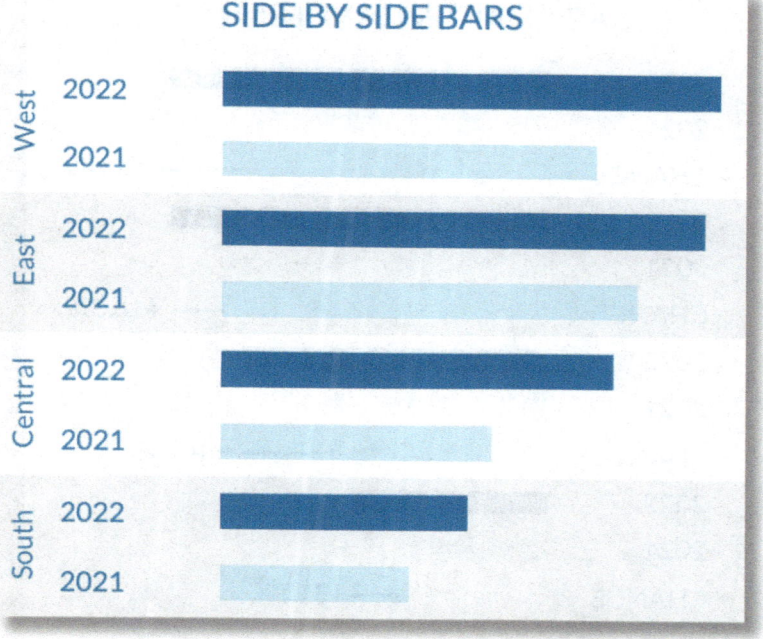

For each region, two periods are compared using differently colored bars.

17

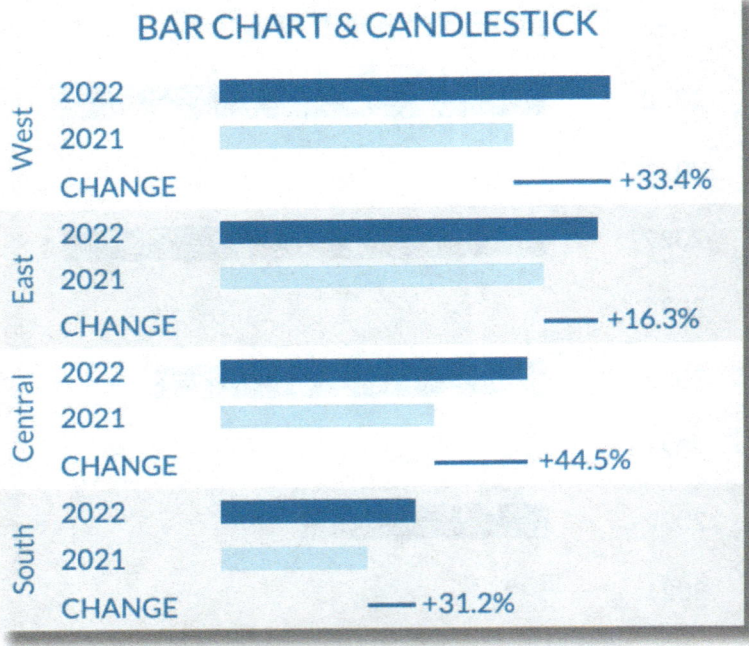

Add a candlestick and label to show the difference between two periods for each region.

18

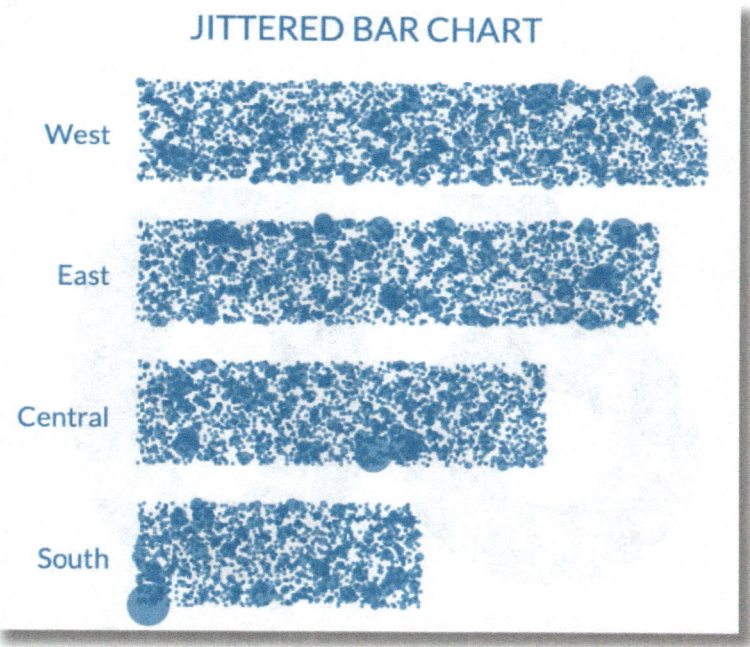

Include every single data point using a jittered bar chart.

The length of the bar represents the total for each region.

60
WAYS TO VISUALIZE TIME

01

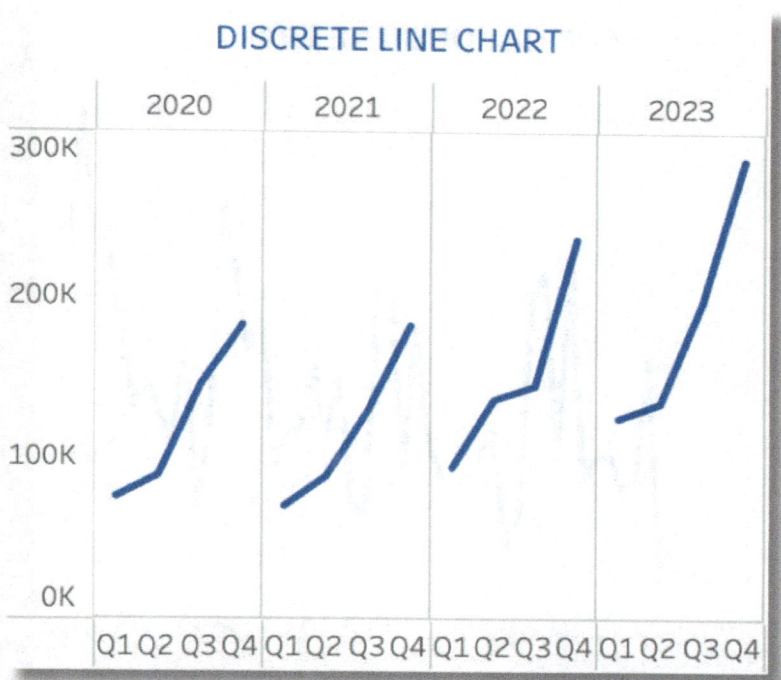

Connect dimension members with a line to show quarterly performance across years.

02

CONTINUOUS LINE CHART

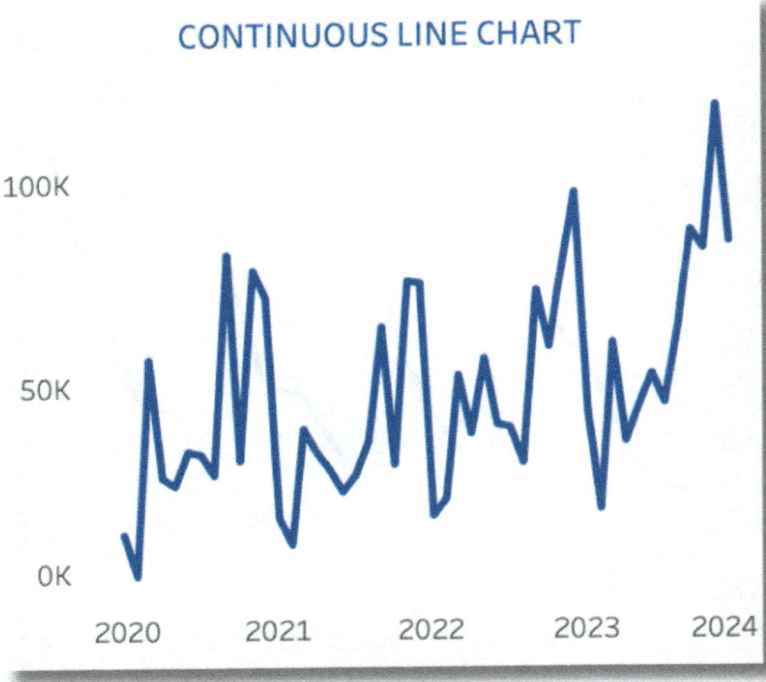

Show trends over time with a single, continuous line.

03

LINE CHART WITH MARKERS

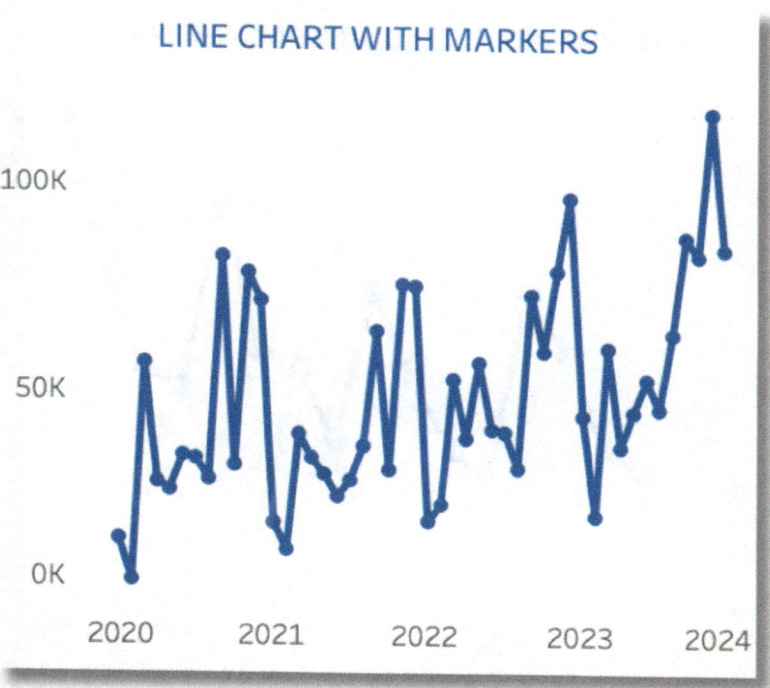

Add markers to highlight the individual data points.

04

LINE CHART WITH CIRCLE MARKERS

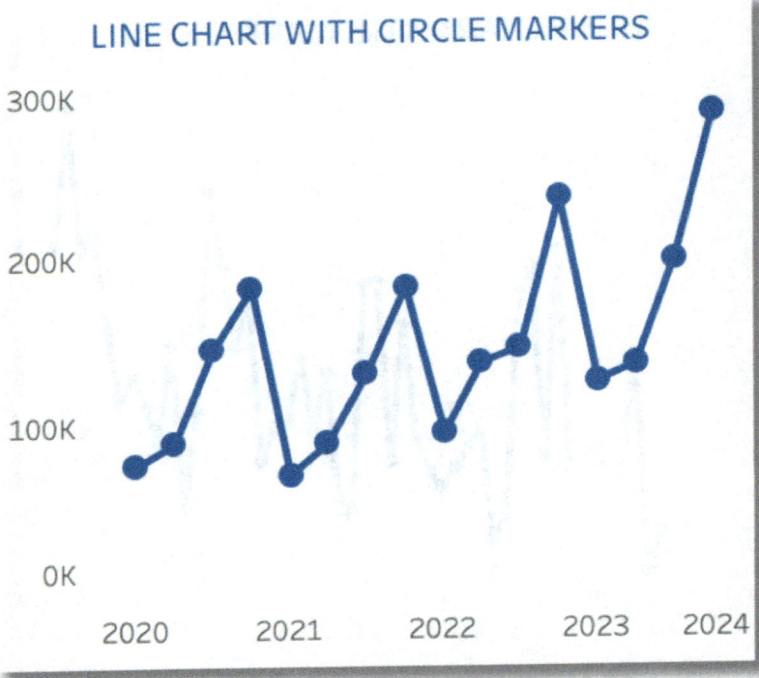

Duplicate the measure to layer larger circles on top of the line.

05

DASHED LINE CHART

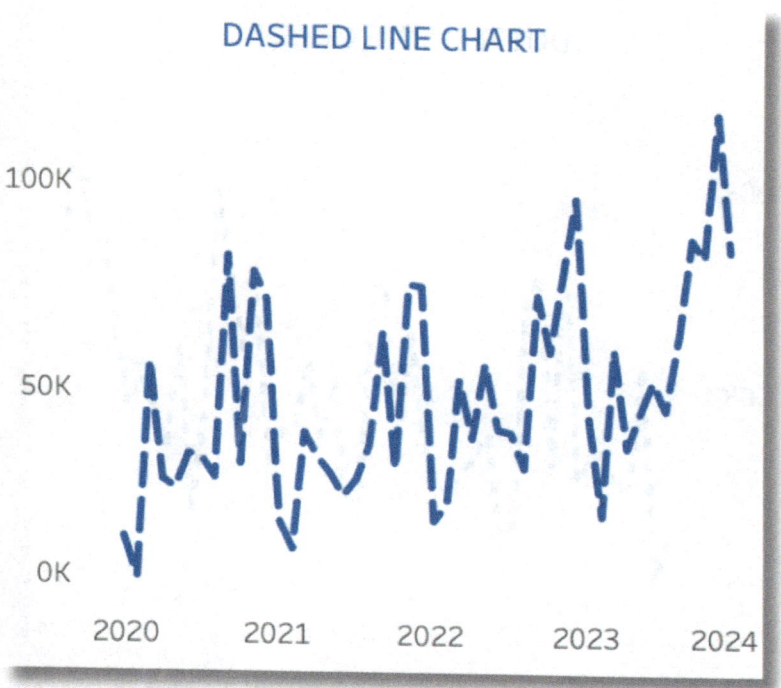

Use dashed lines for a more "broken" look, but beware that this could be misunderstood as missing data.

06

DOTTED LINE CHART

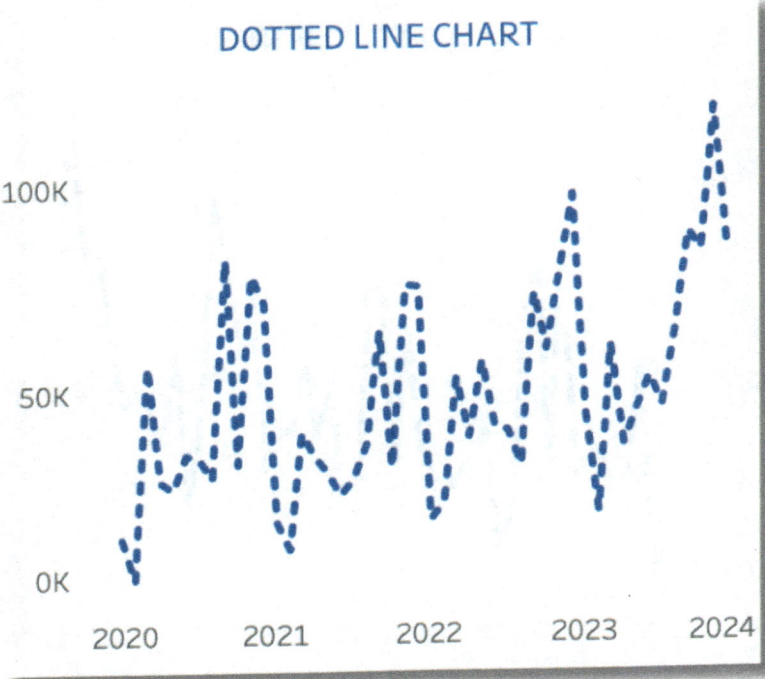

A dotted line still shows the overall trend clearly while giving you an additional design element.

07

STEPPED LINE CHART

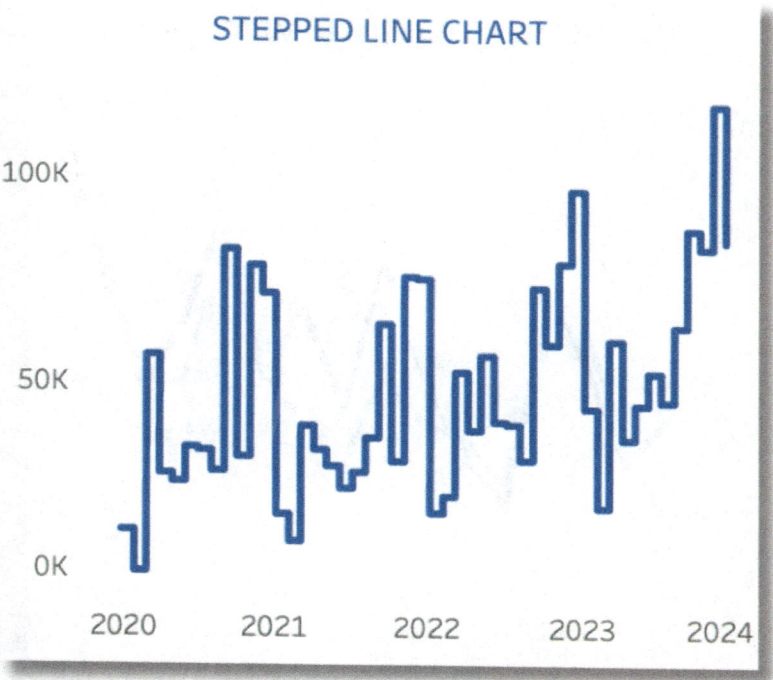

Stepped lines create a 'skyline' effect.

It's similar connecting the tops of a bar chart.

08

LINE CHART MULTIPLE DIMENSIONS

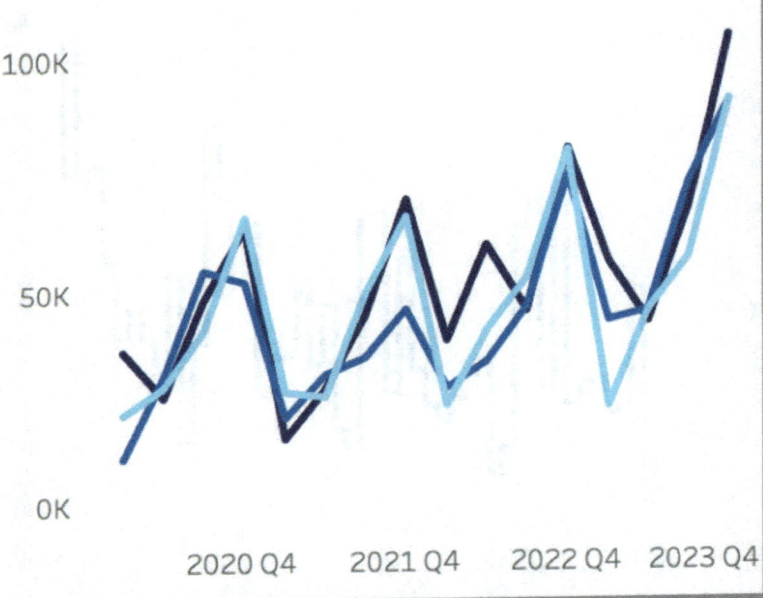

Display a separate line in a different color for each dimension member to compare performance over time.

09

LINE CHART MULTIPLE MEASURES

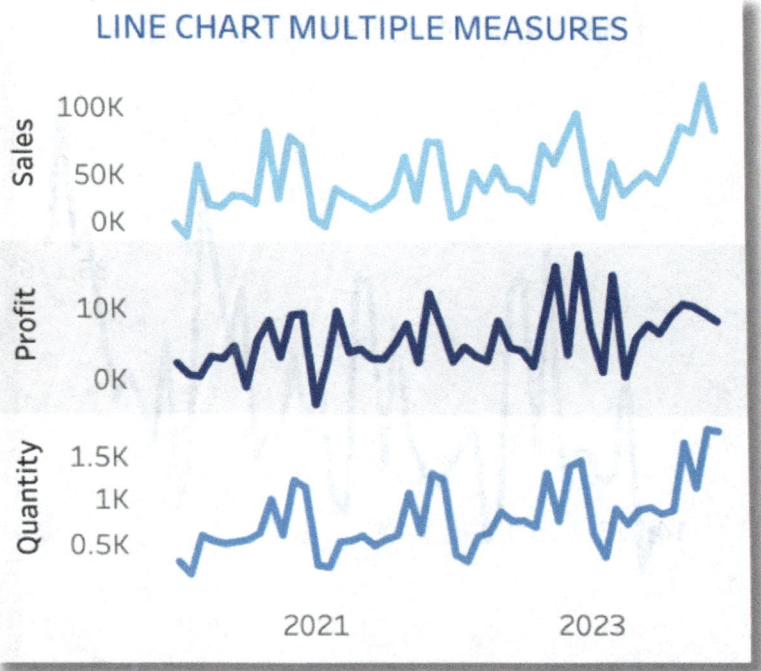

Show trends over time for multiple measures in the same chart, using color to differentiate the measures.

Add background shading to more clearly separate the different areas in your chart.

10

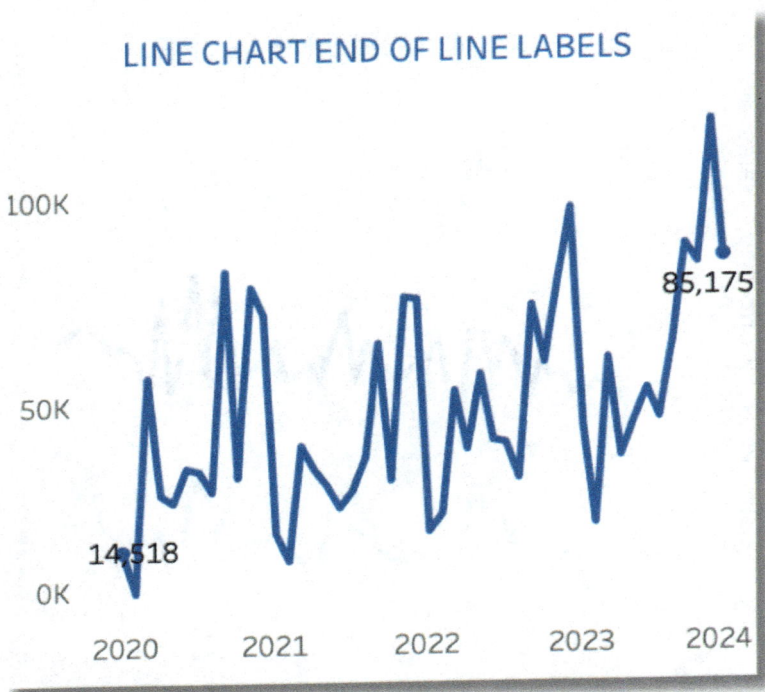

Label the start and end of your line chart for additional context.

11

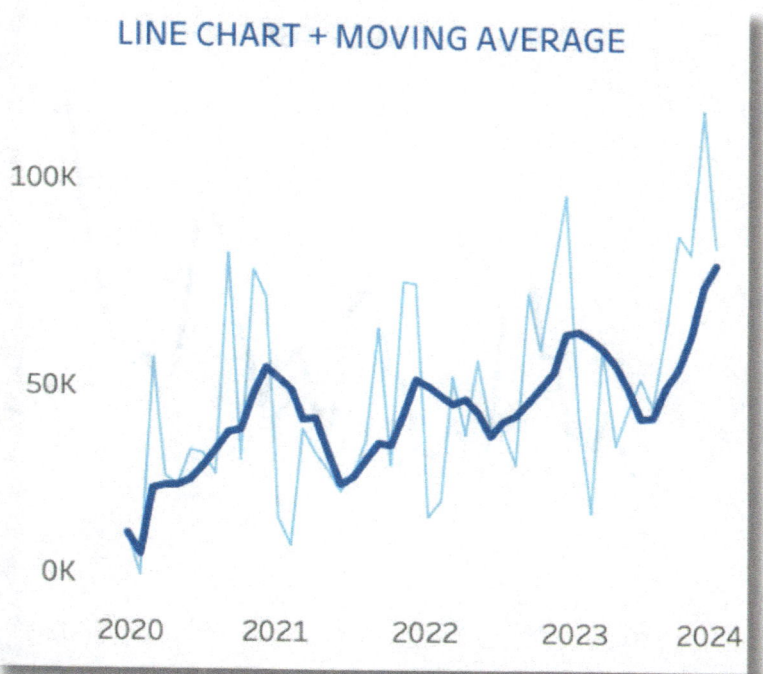

Add a moving average to your line chart to smooth the variability in the data.

12

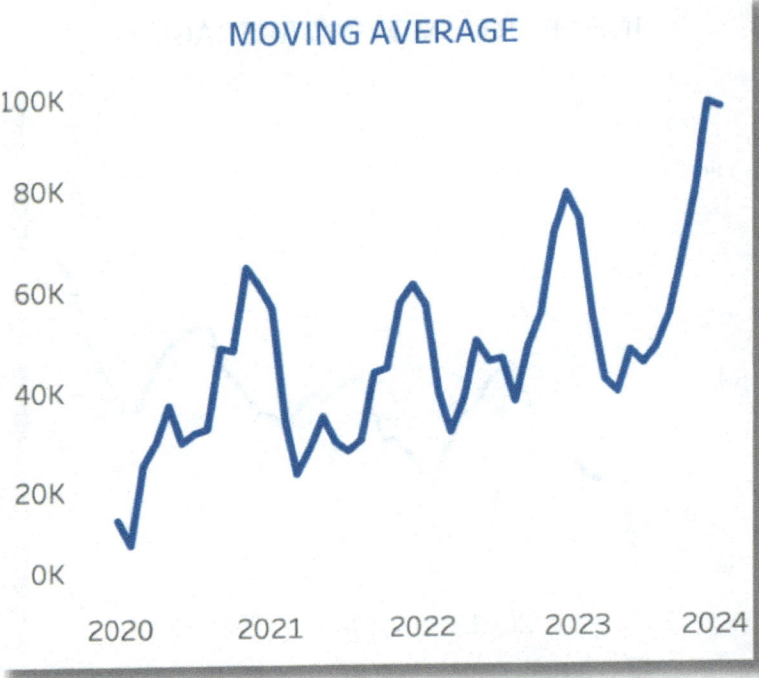

Displaying only the moving average provides the smoothed value without the context of the actual values.

13

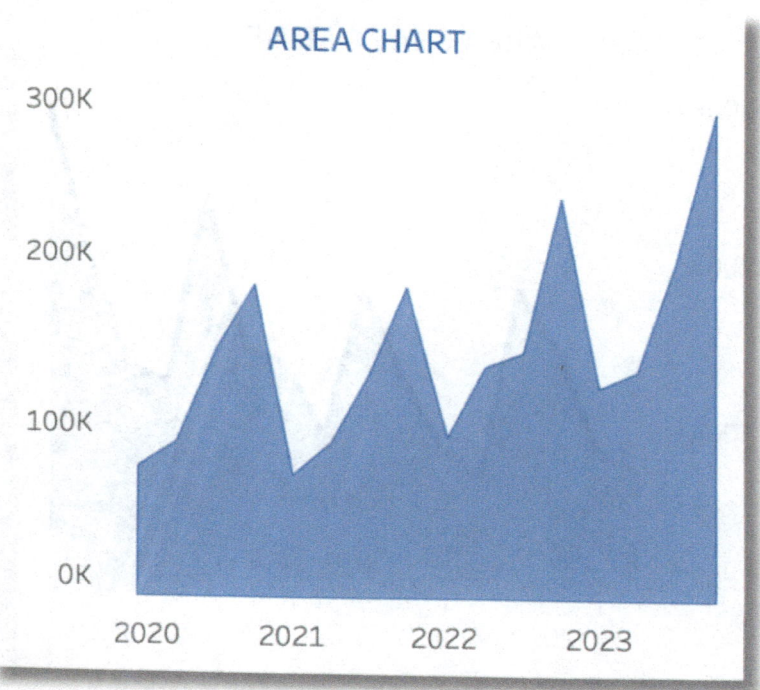

An area chart can be useful for displaying the magnitude of a measure more impactfully.

14

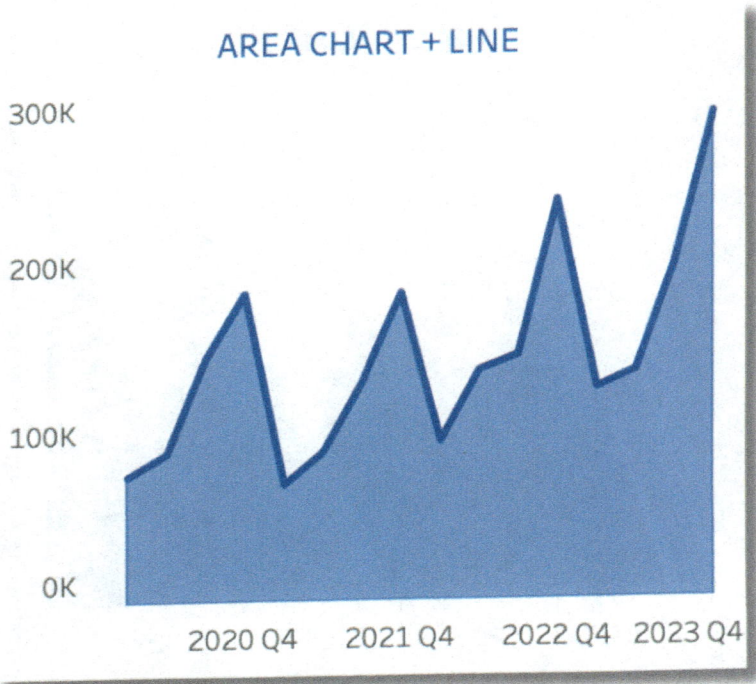

Adding a line to your area chart makes your design look more polished.

15

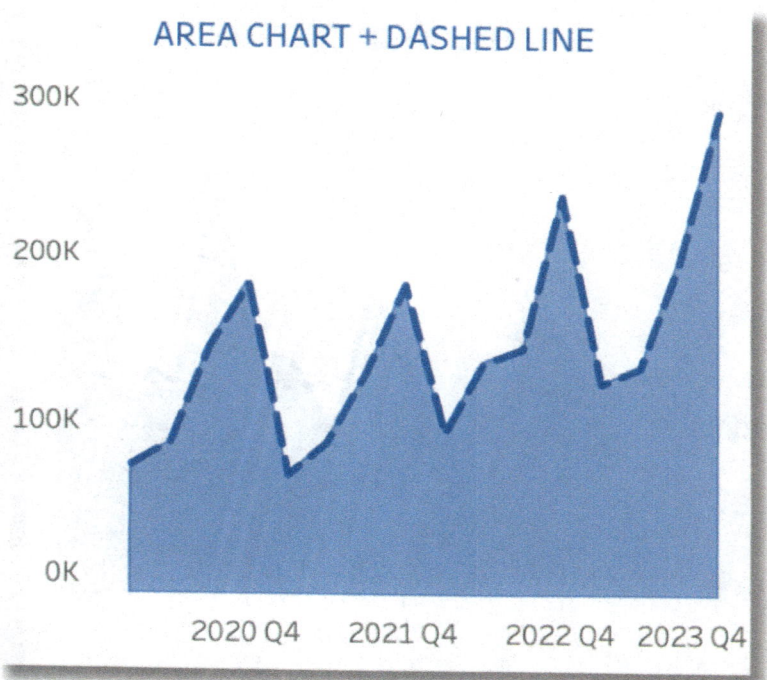

A dashed line on your area chart gives you another visually appealing option.

16

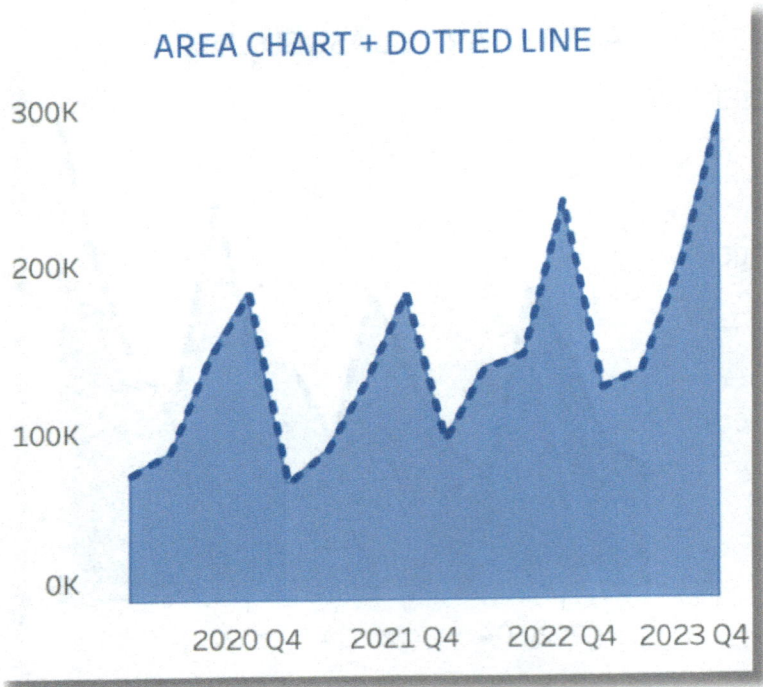

Like the dashed line, a dotted line lets you vary how you display area charts.

17

STACKED AREA CHART

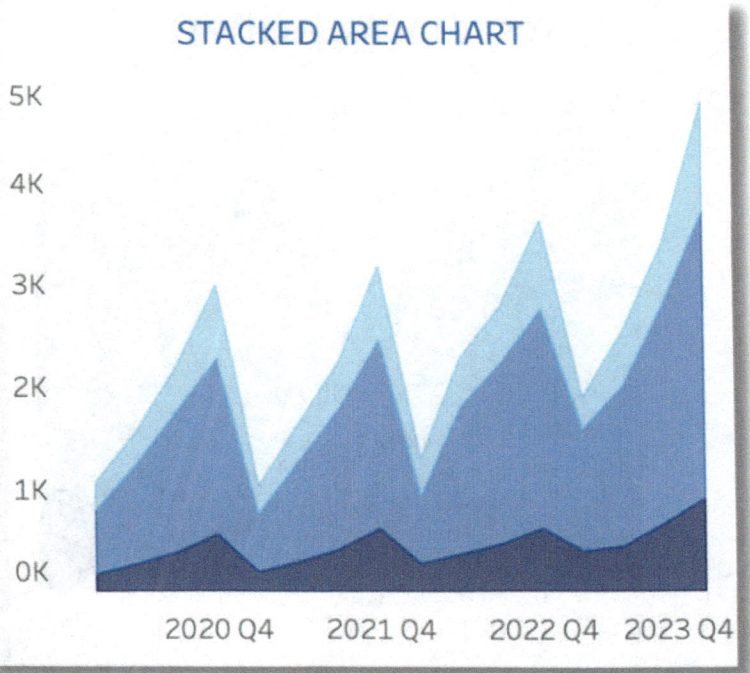

Split your area chart to show each dimension member's contribution to the overall.

18

% OF TOTAL AREA CHART

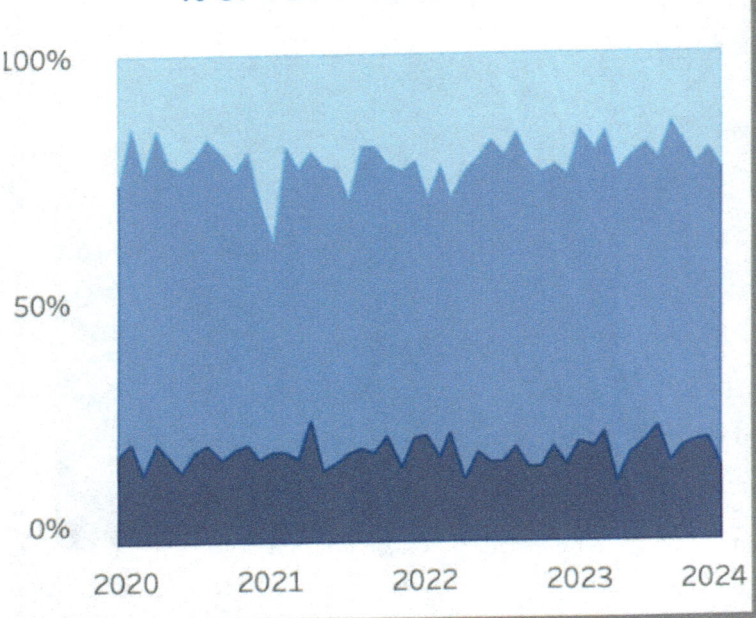

Change your area chart to percentages to show the proportional performance of different regions to overall sales, for example.

19

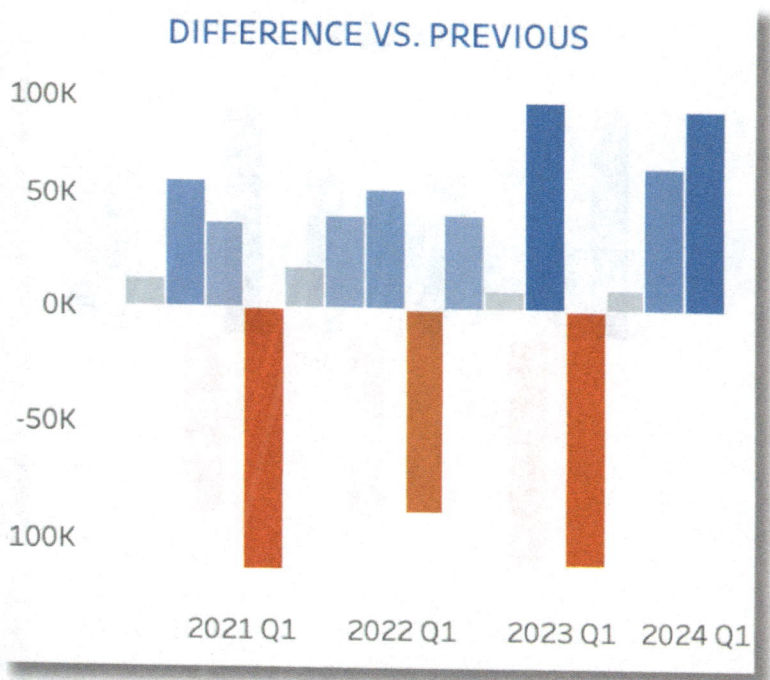

Compare to a previous time period when measuring performance time period after time period is important.

20

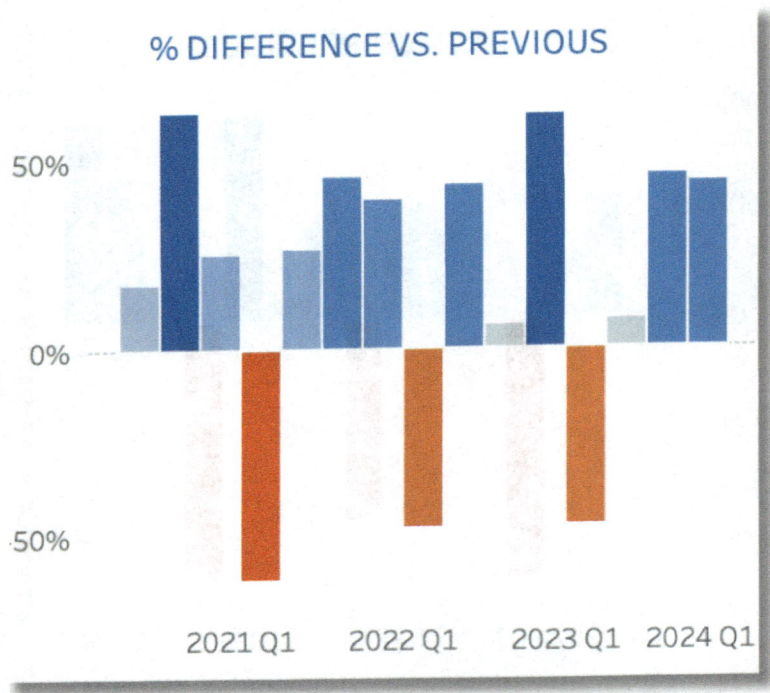

Converting to a percentage changes adds context that could be lost otherwise.

21

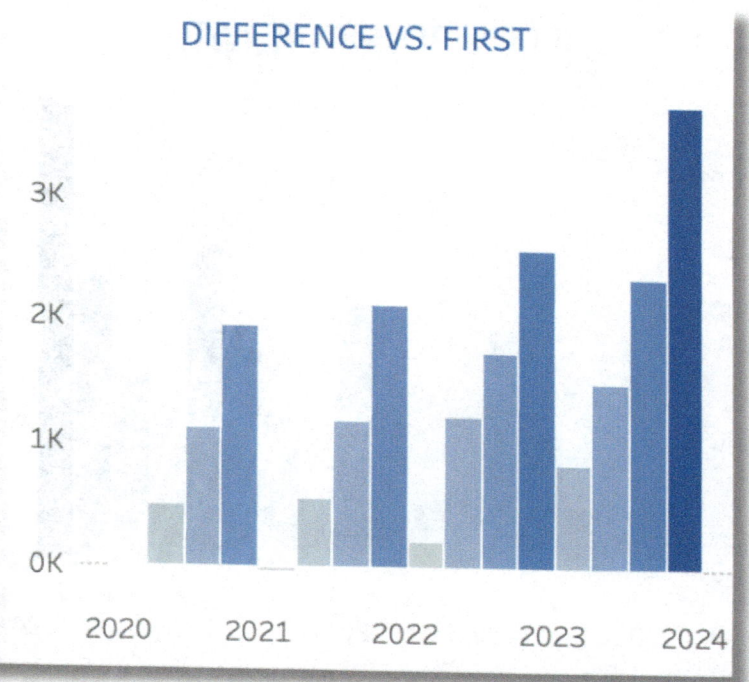

Compare your results to a baseline, e.g. the first time you sold something, to show overall and relative growth.

22

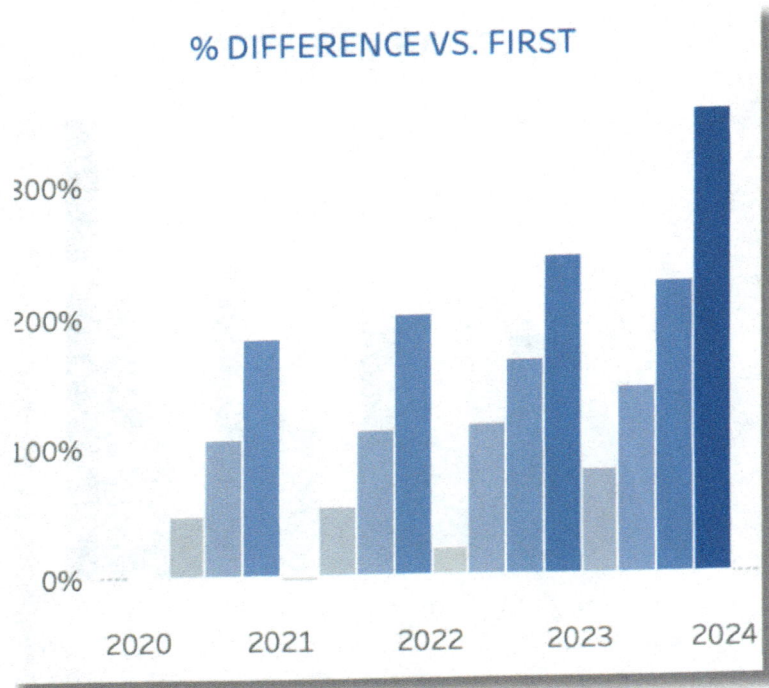

Use percentages to show proportional growth against a common baseline.

23

RUNNING TOTAL

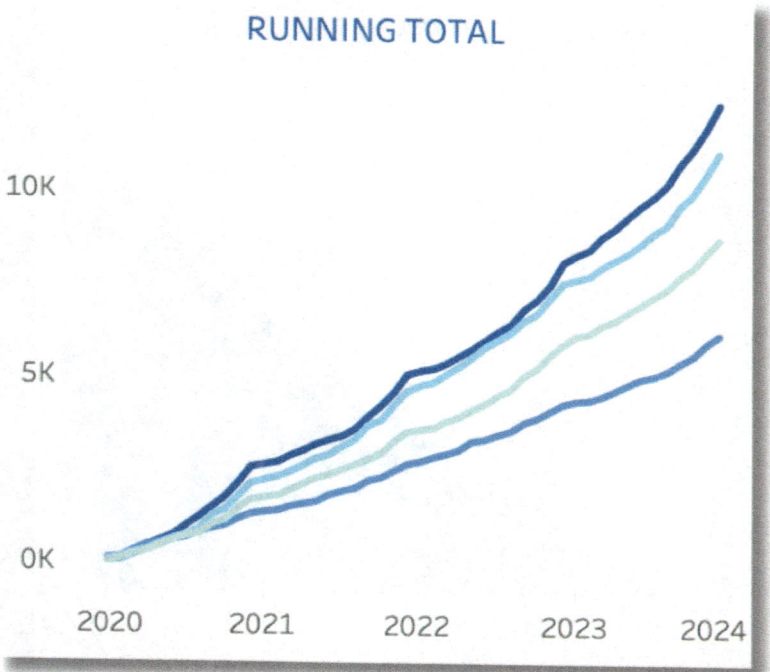

Calculating a running total allows you to compare the growth of products over time.

24

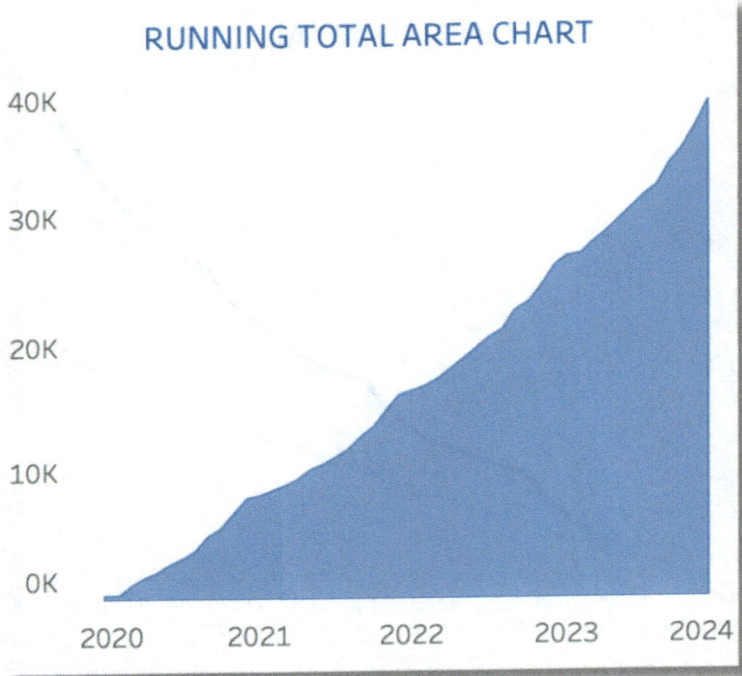

Shading the area under your line helps emphasize the magnitude of the growth.

25

RUNNING TOTAL FROM FIRST SALE

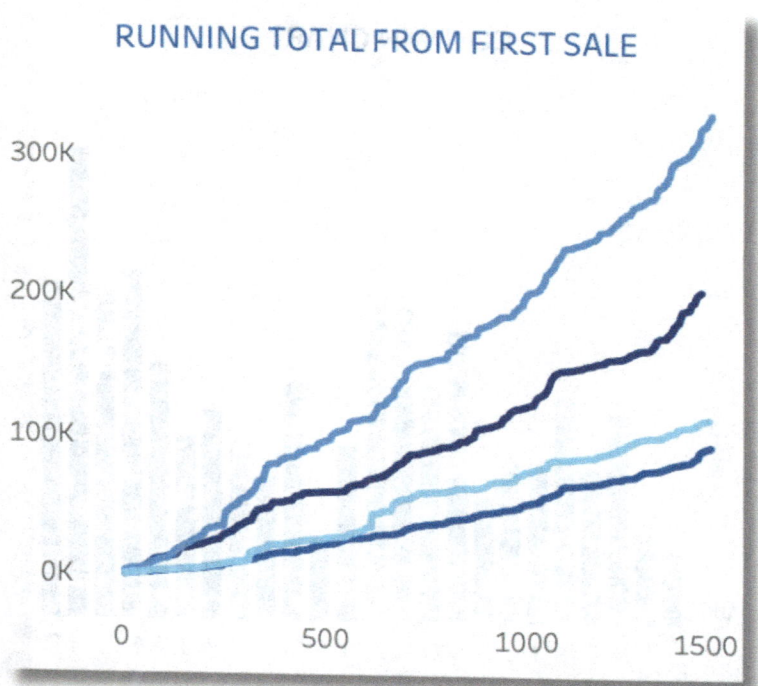

Use first sale as a common baseline to show how different departments or regions have performed since they first started selling.

26

COLUMN CHART

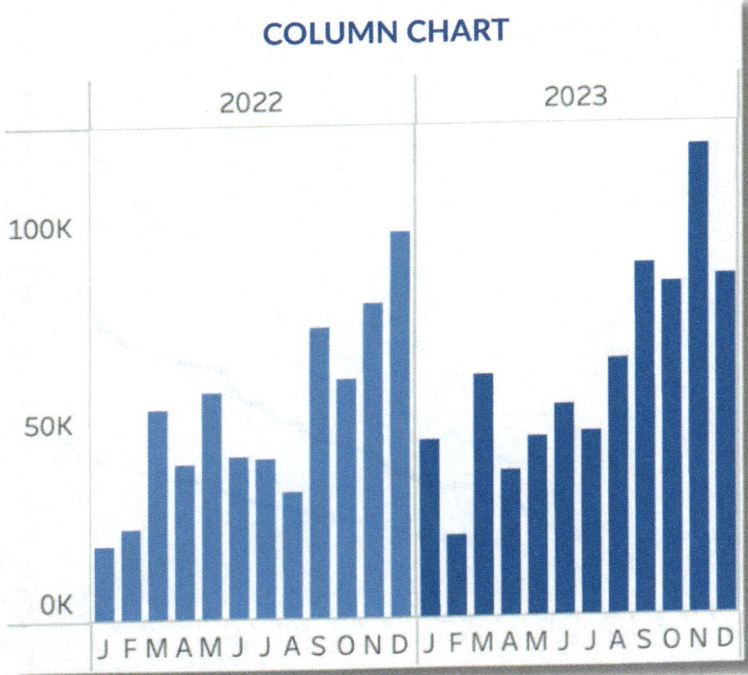

Break down your bar chart into discrete months and years for easy comparison over time.

27

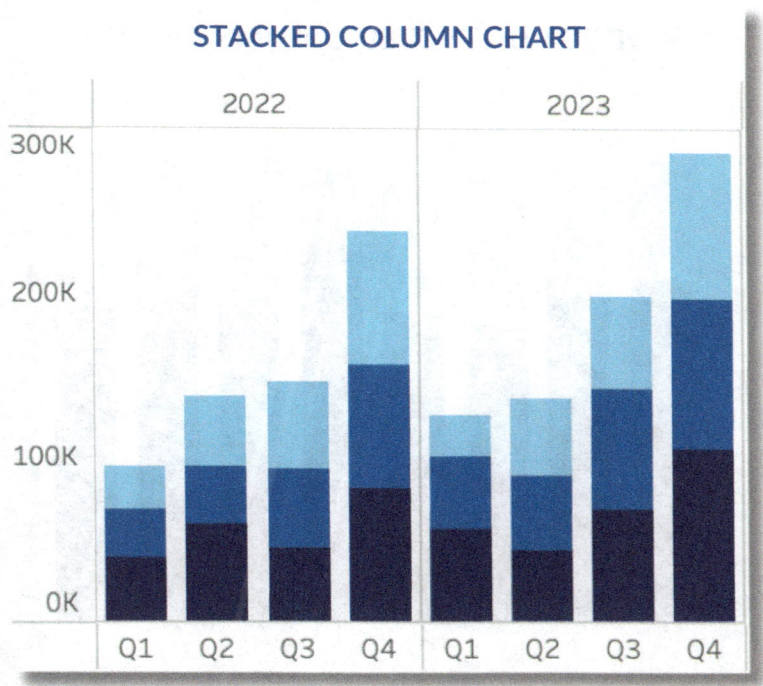

Stack dimension members in a bar chart to show their contribution to quarterly results.

28

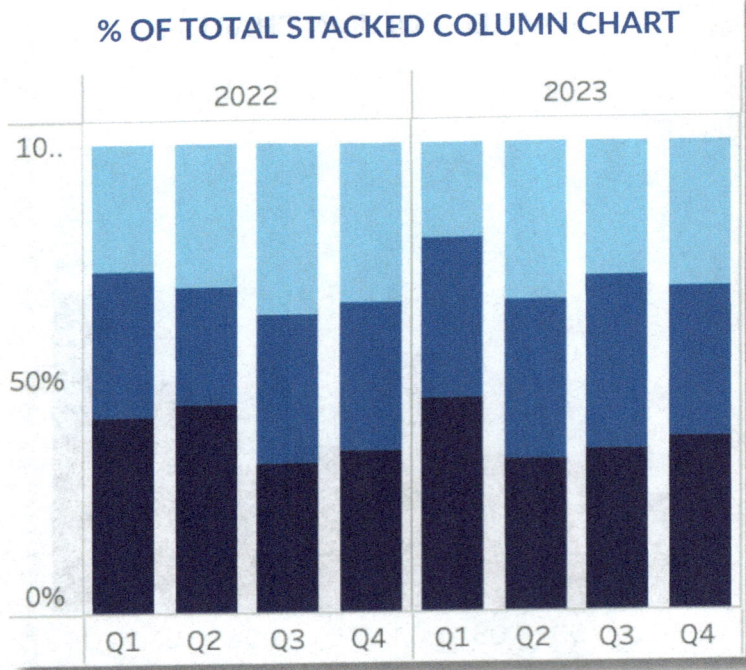

Show proportional contributions over time by using percentages in your stacked bar chart.

29

LOLLIPOP CHART

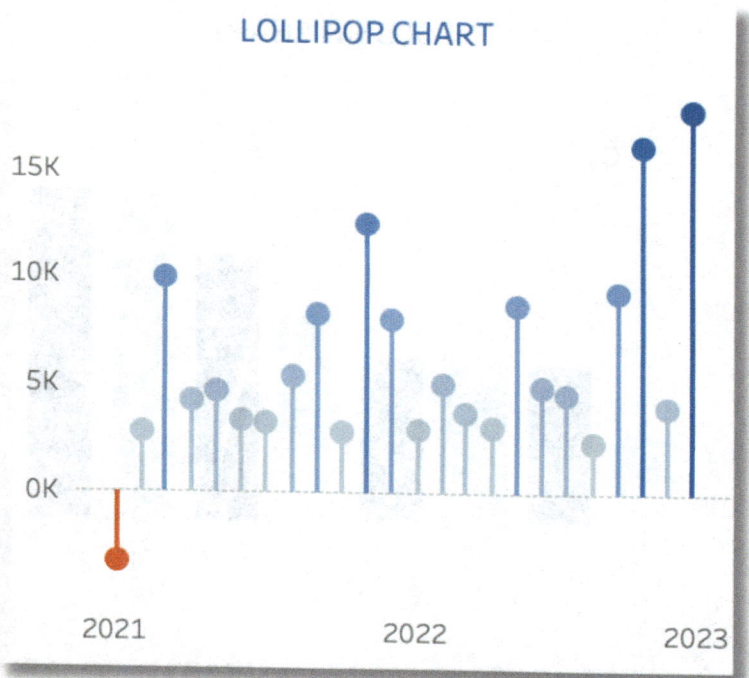

Add circles to the end of thin bars for a lollipop effect.

This chart type allows you to clearly highlight the length of the bar.

30

PAIRED COLUMN CHART

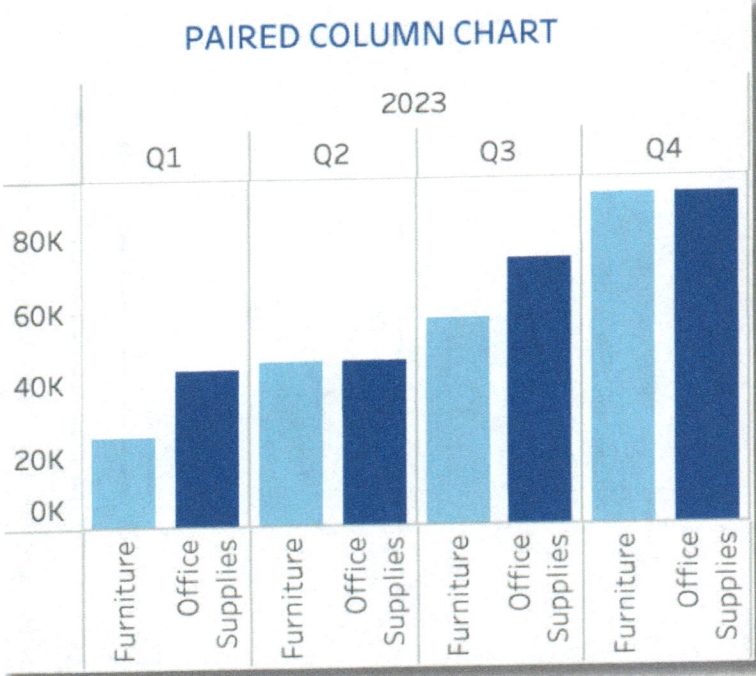

Compare the performance of two dimensions more easily by pairing them side by side.

31

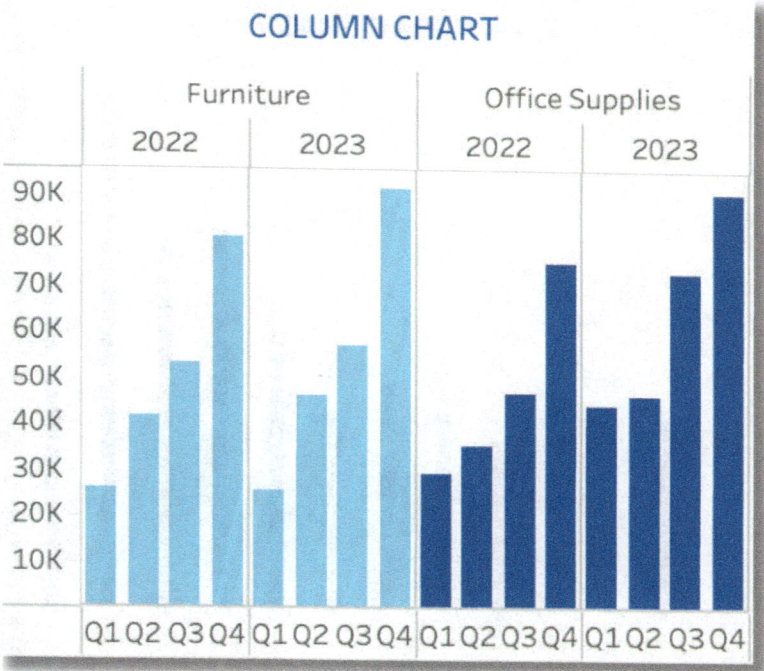

Alternatively, compare the trend of each product separately over time.

32

BAR-IN-BAR CHART

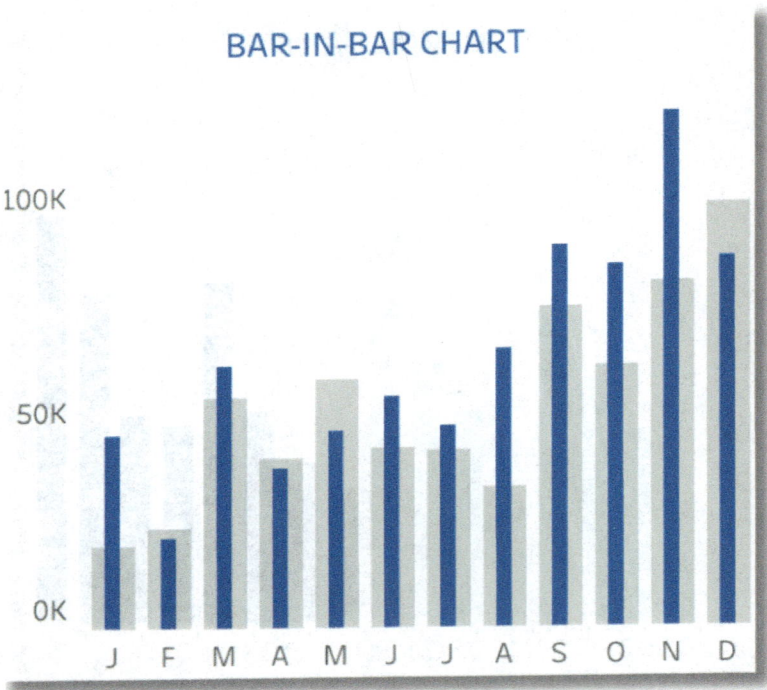

Show sales across the year and compared to a prior period using a bar in bar chart.

33

BAR CHART VS. REFERENCE LINE

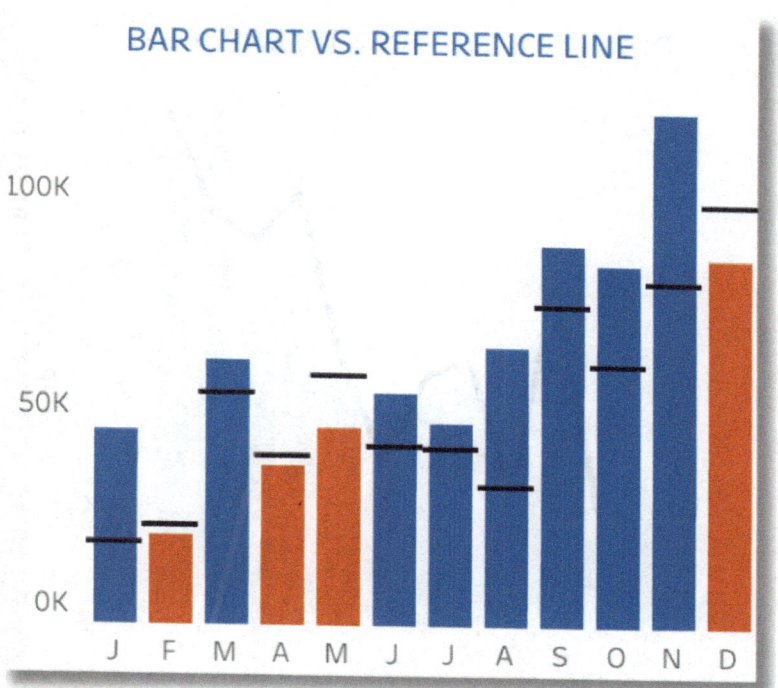

A reference line serves to compare actual vs target or current vs prior year across months.

34

DUAL-AXIS DIFFERENT MEASURES

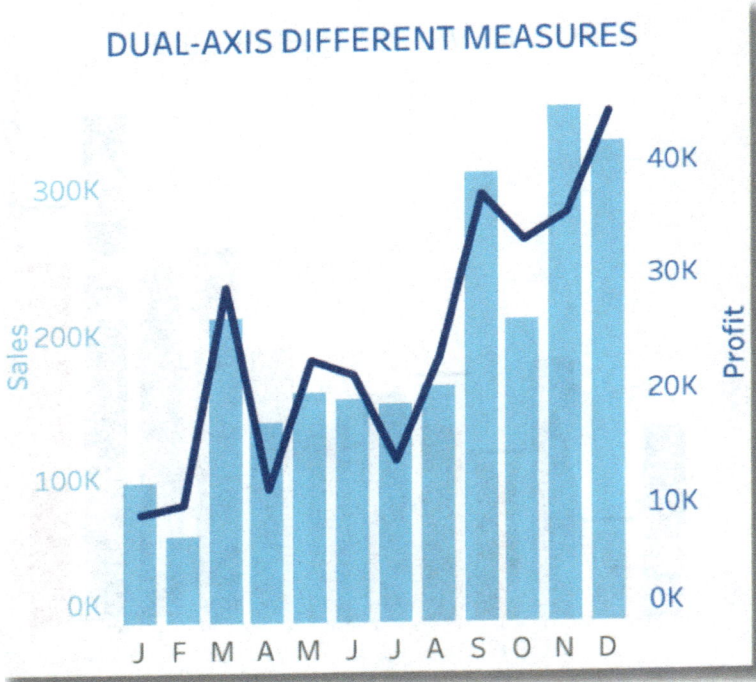

Combine two unrelated measures in a single chart and display one as bars, the other as a line to look for common patterns.

35

DUAL-AXIS RELATED MEASURES

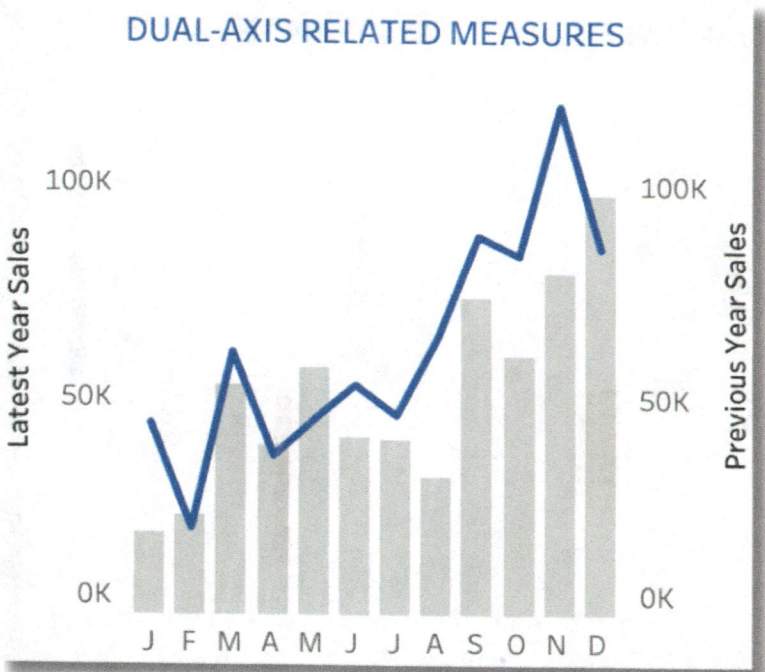

Create two related measures and compare them on the same scale as two different chart types.

36

VARIANCE TO OVERALL AVERAGE BAR CHART

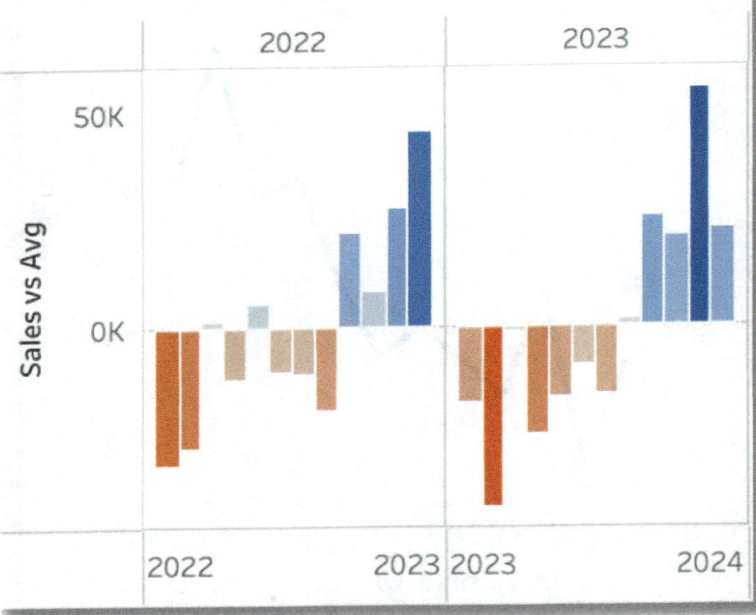

Use the overall average as a baseline for assessing sales for each month across two years.

37

VARIANCE TO PANE AVERAGE BAR CHART

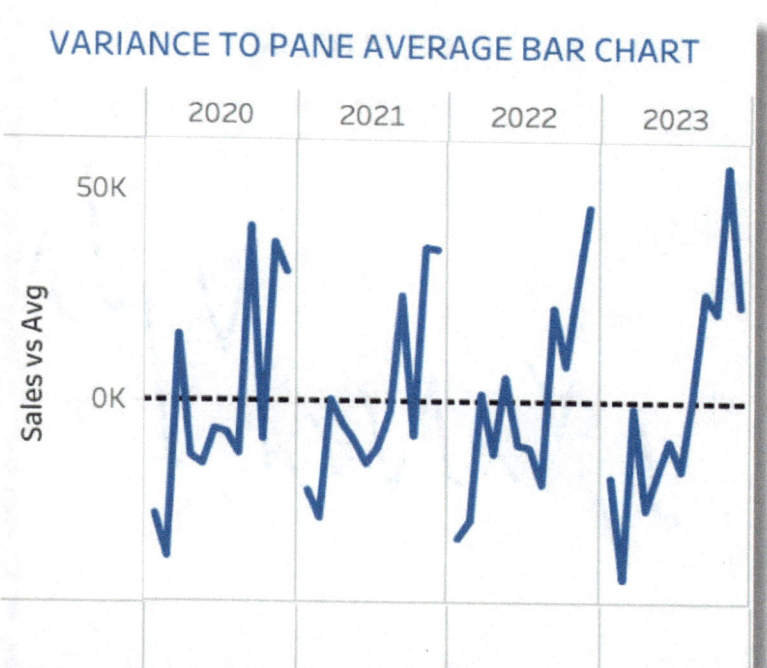

Alternatively, use lines however the positive or negative variance is difficult to see.

38

CYCLE PLOT

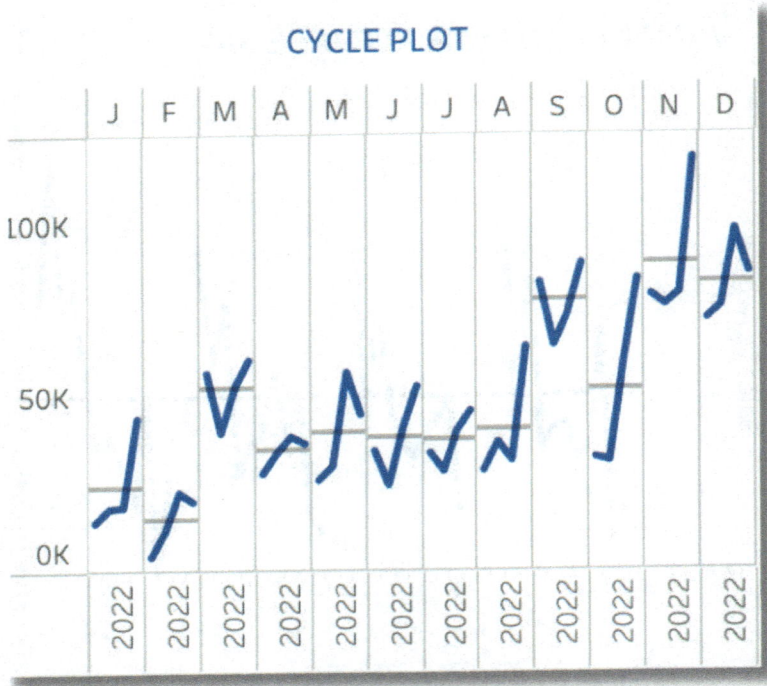

A cycle plot lets you display a trend across multiple years for each individual month.

Add a reference line for additional context.

39

CALENDAR MONTH

Mon	Tue	Wed	Thu	Fri	Sat	Sun
				1	2	3
4	5	6	7	8	9	10
11		13	14	15	16	17
18	19	20	21	22	23	24
25	26	27	28	29	30	

Use a calendar view to show data at the daily level in a familiar format.

40

DISCRETE SLOPE GRAPH

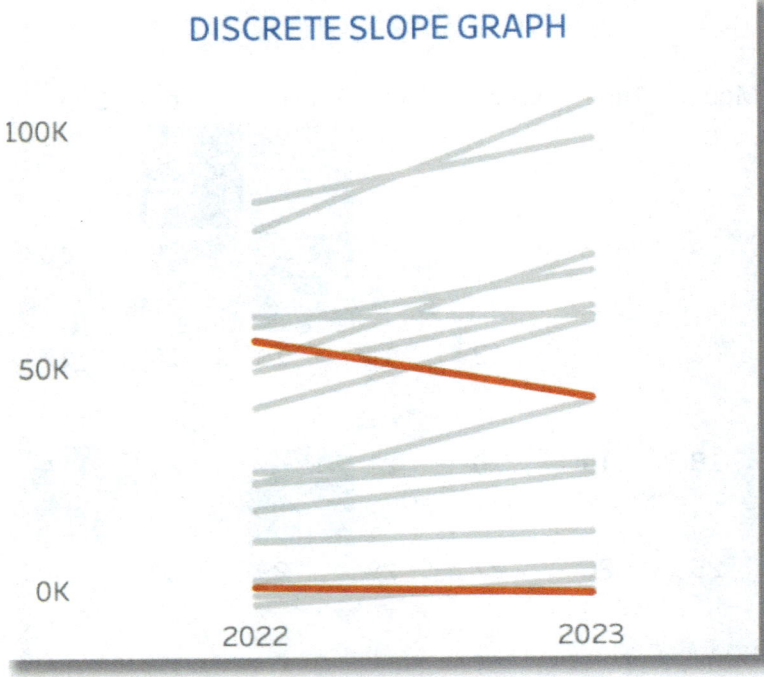

Display months in a slope chart across two years to show increases or decreases over time.

41

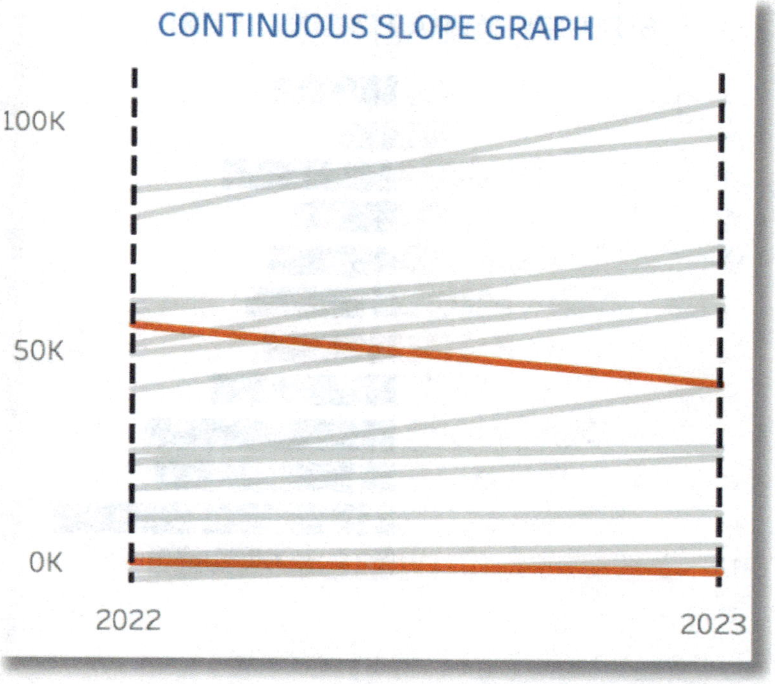

CONTINUOUS SLOPE GRAPH

A continuous slope chart gives you axes to anchor your lines.

42

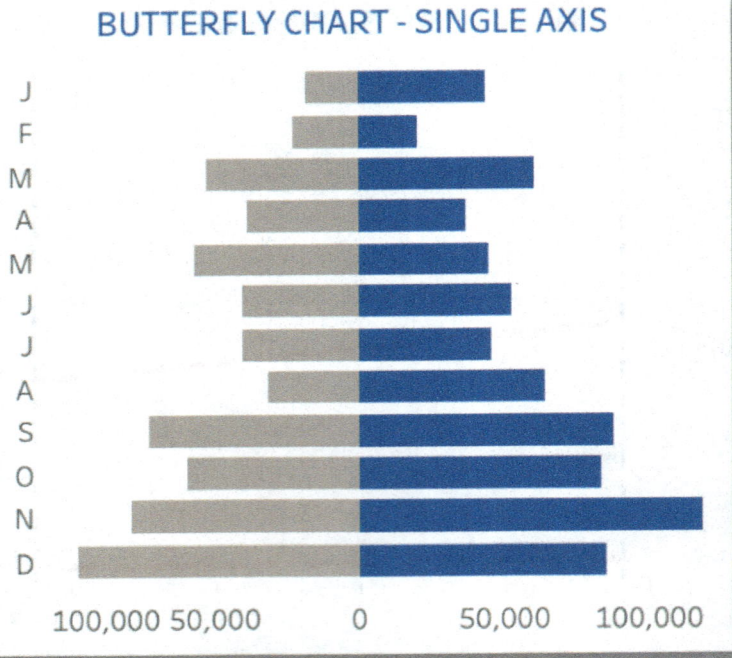

BUTTERFLY CHART - SINGLE AXIS

Display two time series in opposite directions on the same axis. The scale with automatically adjust appropriately.

43

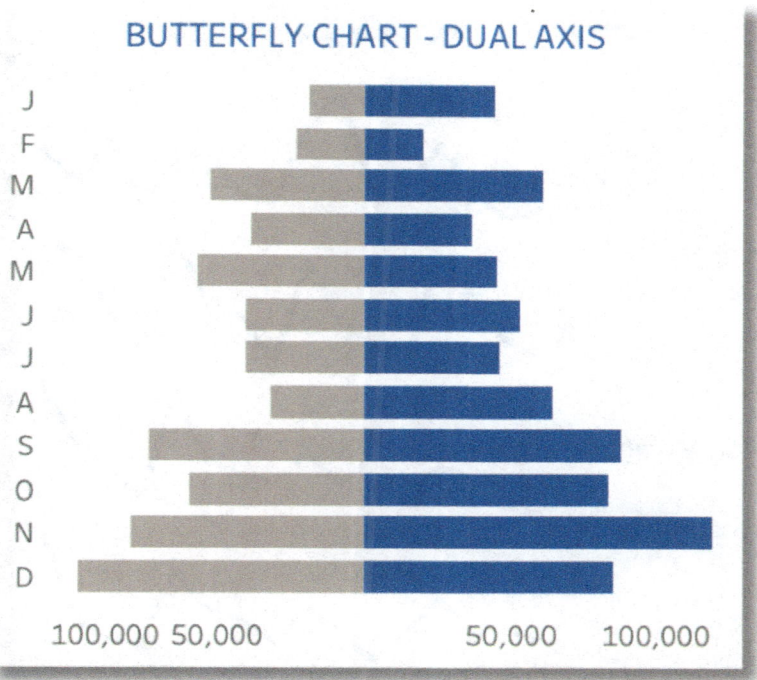

Similar to the previous example, but using two axes. Be sure to use the same scale on both axes.

44

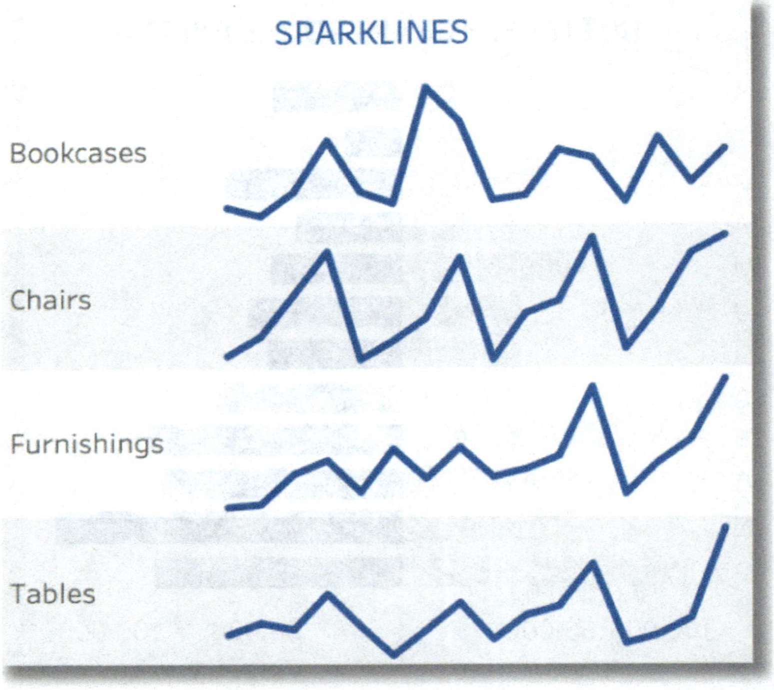

Visualize trends over time with small lines that add a quick overview.

45

SPARKBARS

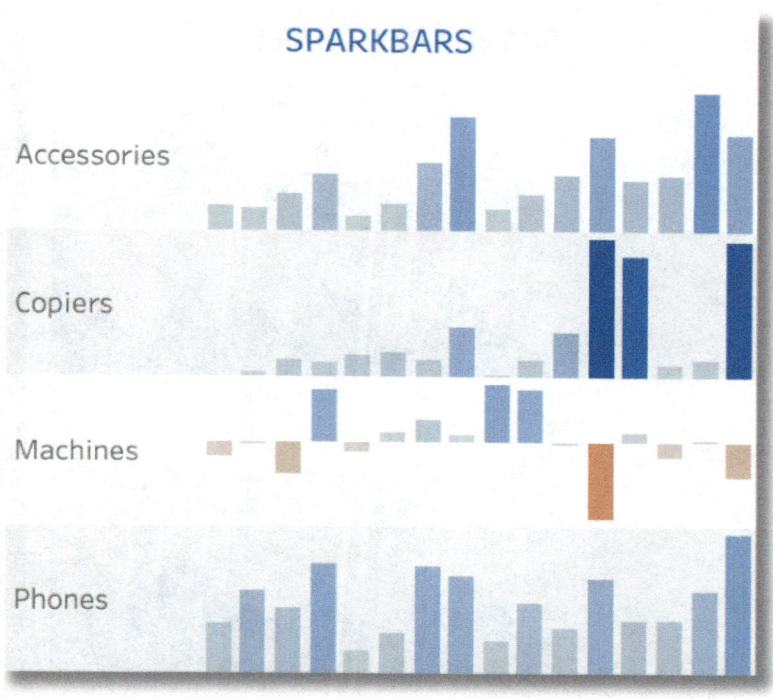

Like sparklines, sparkbars give a quick view of trends over time.

Add color for additional context.

46

SPARK AREA CHART

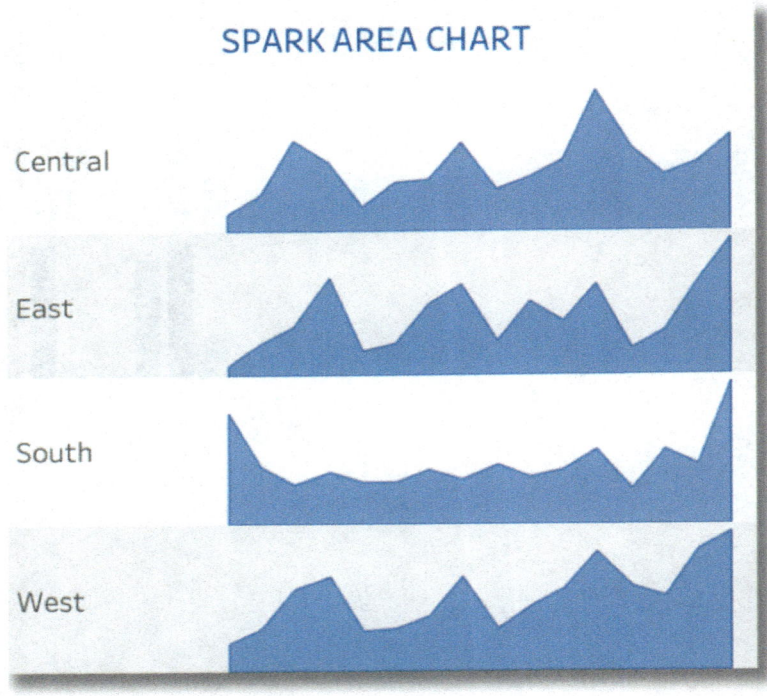

Shade the area under your sparklines to highlight peaks and troughs.

Ensure the axis starts at zero.

47

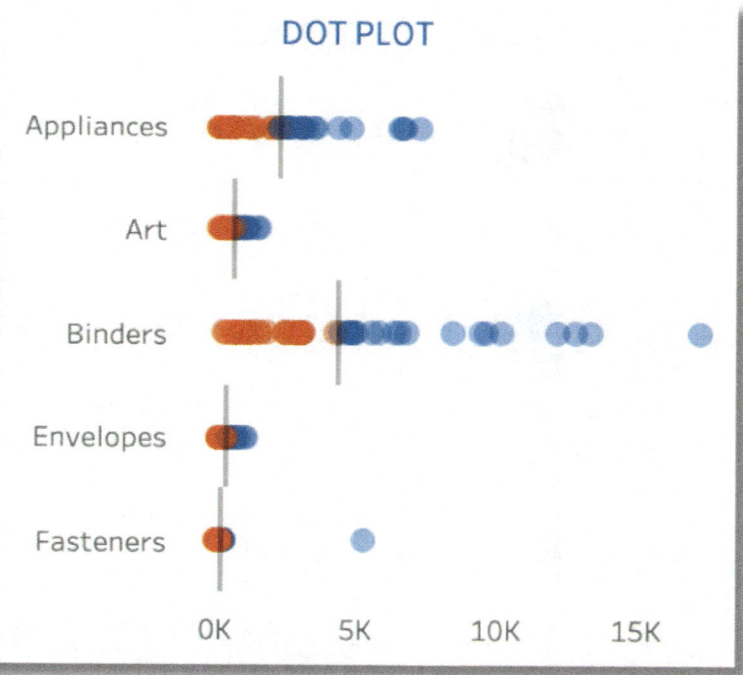

Include data points for each time period in a dot plot to show those months that were below vs above a target or average.

48

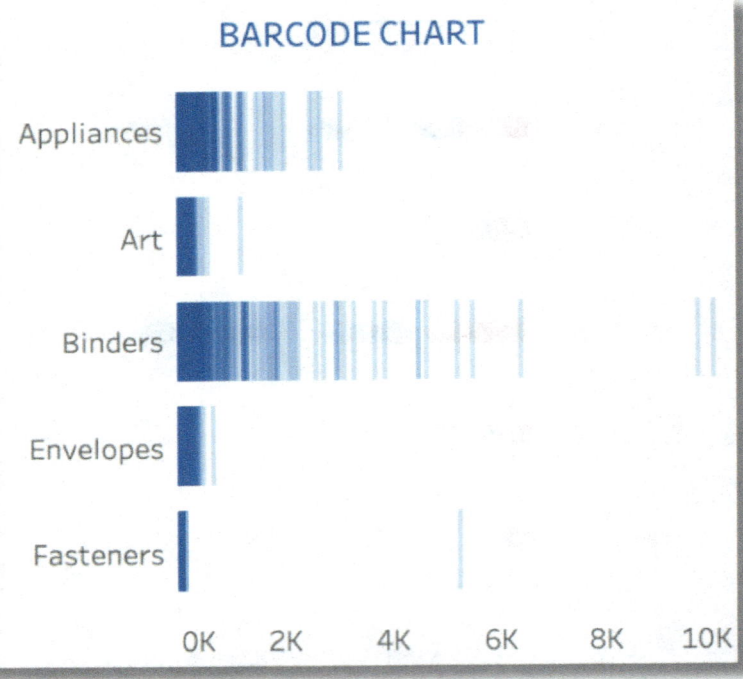

Display extremely detailed data using a barcode chart to identify clusters and concentrations.

49

CONNECTED DOT PLOT

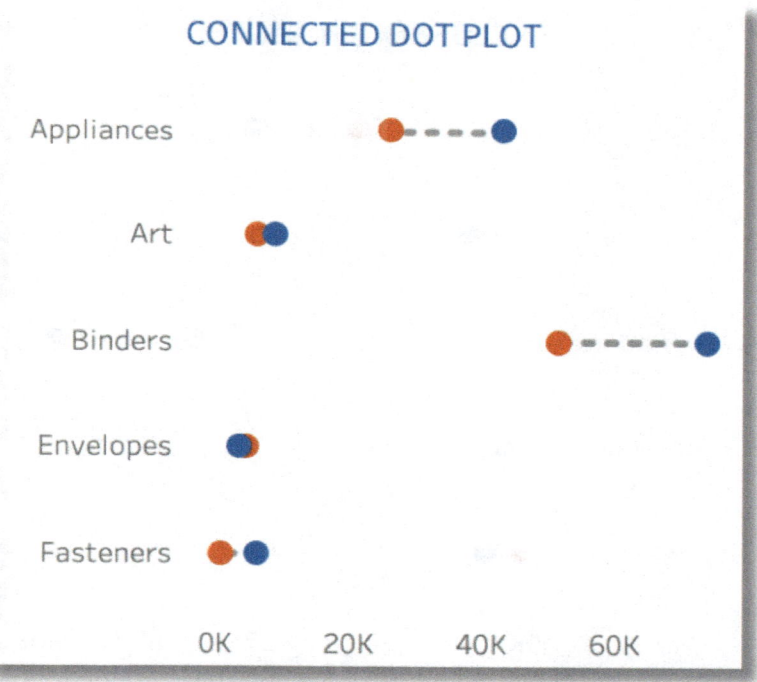

Connect two data points, e.g. prior and current year, for each category with a line to highlight variance.

50

ENCLOSED DOT PLOT

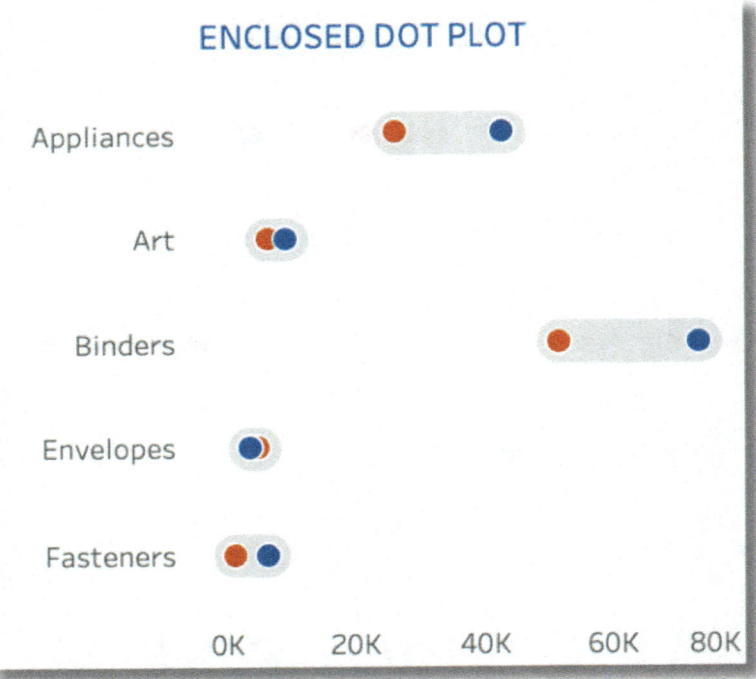

Enclose the gap between two data points and add shading to highlight the difference between two years.

51

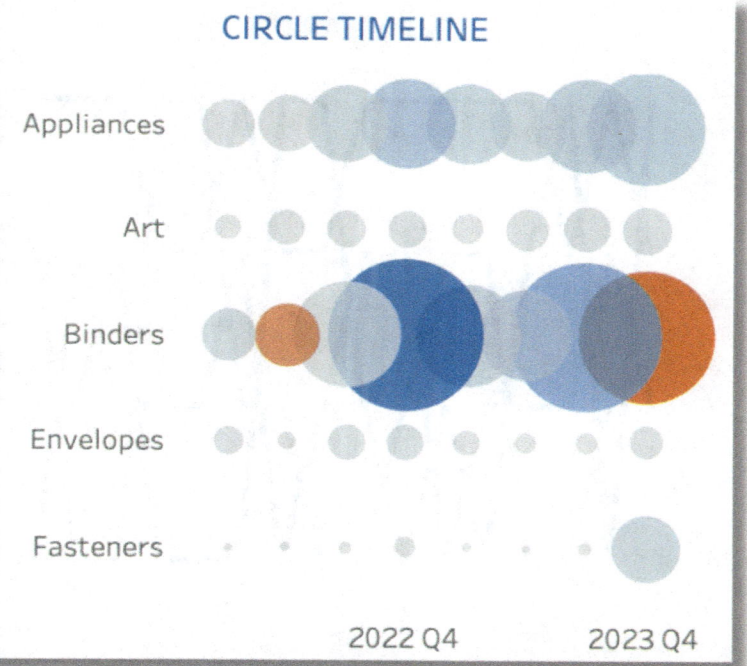

Good for showing discrete values of varying size across multiple categories.

52

BUMP CHART

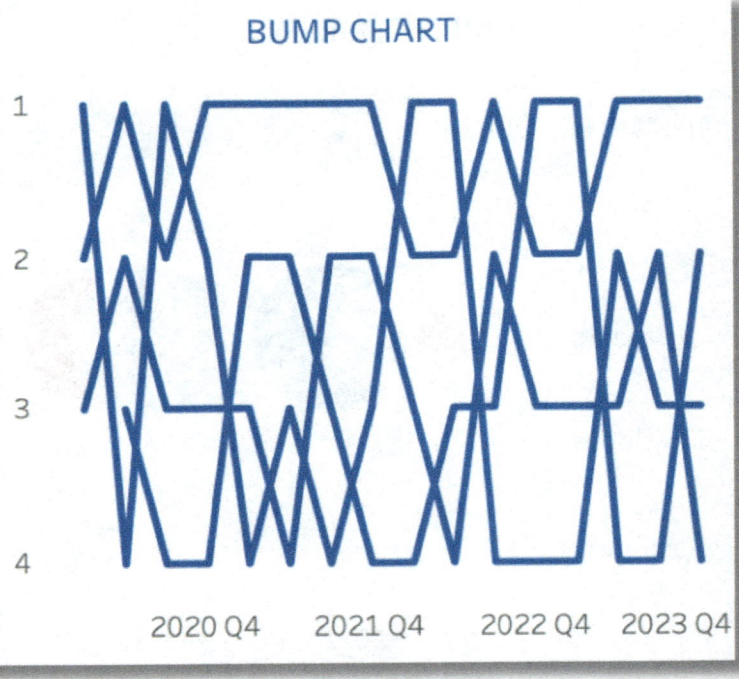

Rank the performance of a dimension members over time.

53

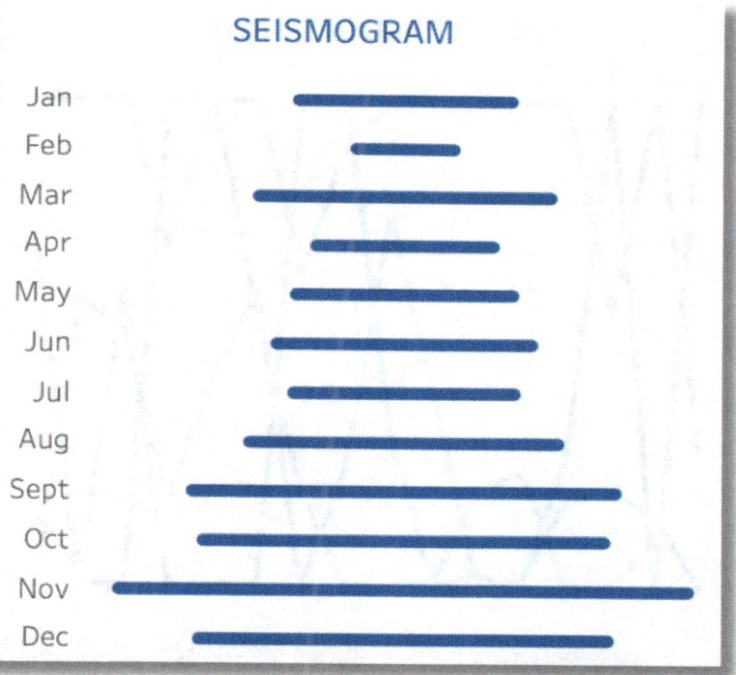

SEISMOGRAM

An alternative to the circle timeline for showing series where there are big variations in the data.

54

PARALLEL COORDINATES

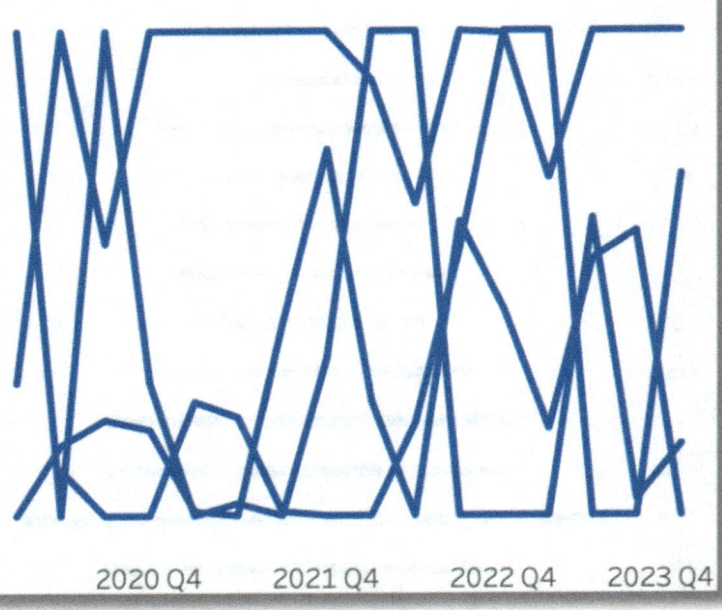

Similar to a rank chart exception the variance is shown as a percentage from the maximum value on a 0-100 scale.

55

SMALL MULTIPLE DONUT CHART

Show parts to the whole using a simple donut chart that breaks data down into quarters and years for easy comparison

56

CONNECTED SCATTERPLOT

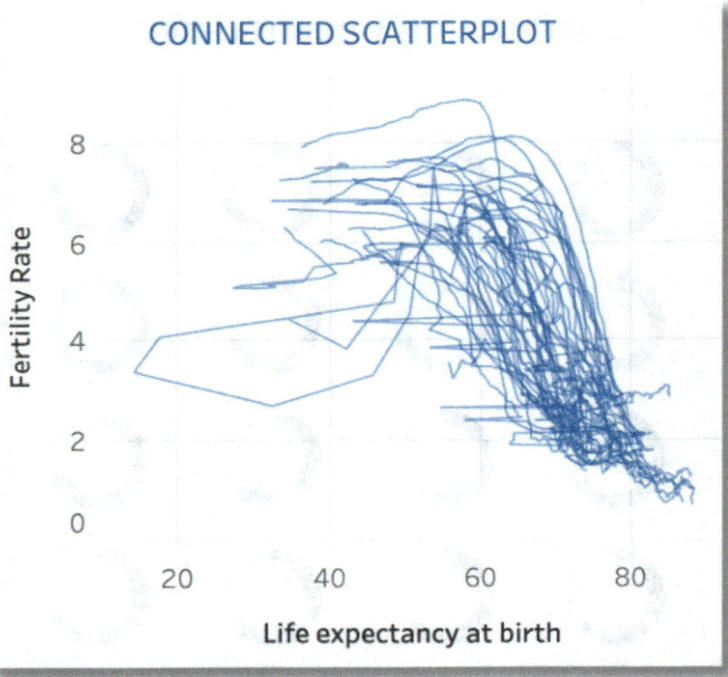

Show an overall trend in two metrics over time by connecting the data points in your scatterplot.

57

CONNECTED SCATTERPLOT DOTTED LINES

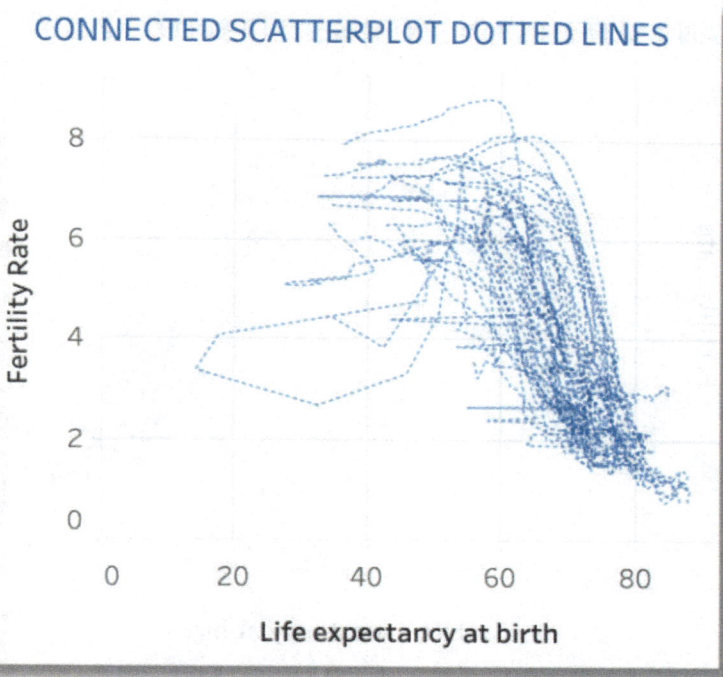

Dotted lines enhance the perception of movement in the data.

58

ANIMATED CONNECTED SCATTERPLOT - 2021

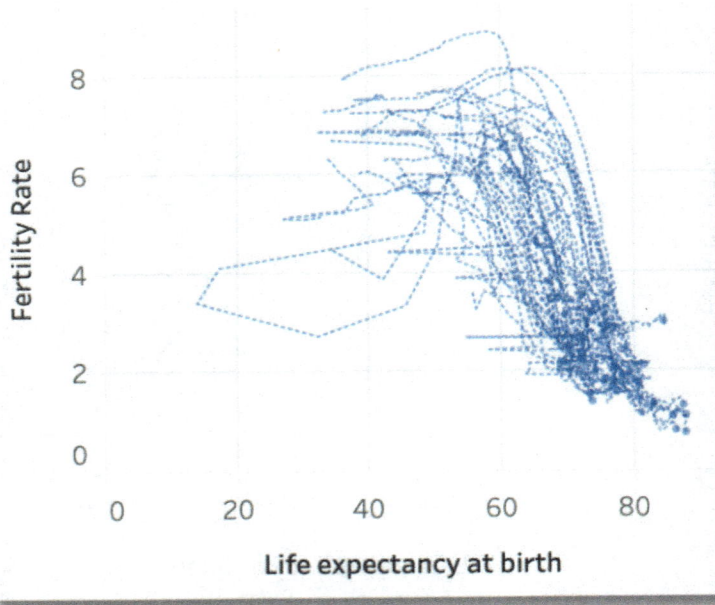

Animate your connected scatterplot so viewers can see trends appear.

59

WATERFALL CHART

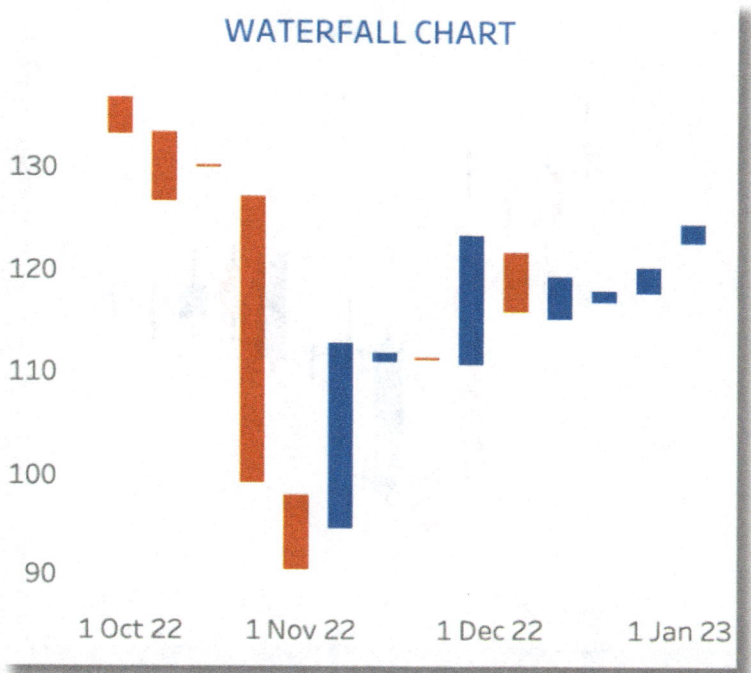

Use a waterfall chart to show decreases and increases over time, using each previous data point as the start for the next bar.

60

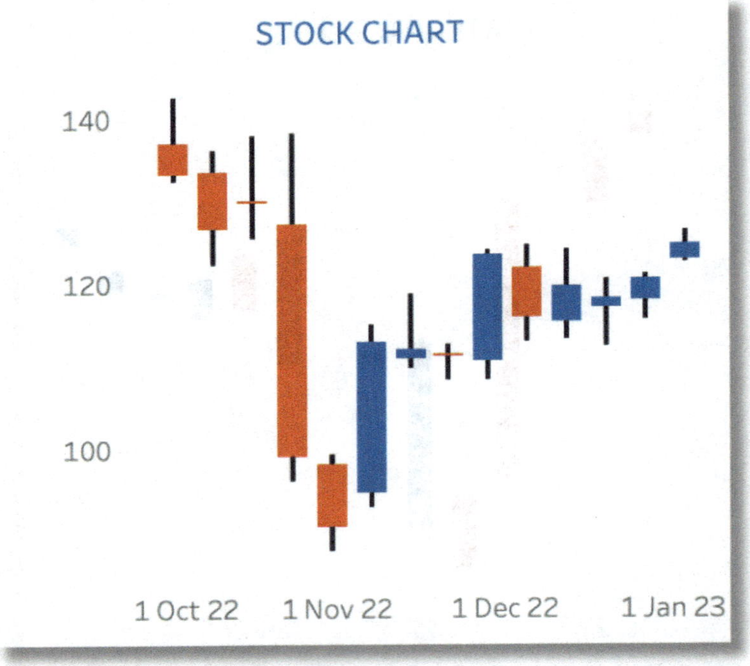

STOCK CHART

Usually focused on day-to-day activity, a stock chart shows opening/closing and high/low points of each day.

FOLLOW AND CONNECT

 andykriebel.com

 nextleveltableau.com

 LinkedIn

Made in the USA
Monee, IL
03 July 2024